Seed Bead
Chic

seed Bead
Chic

25 elegant projects
inspired by fine jewelry

Amy Katz

LARK JEWELRY
& BEADING

Credits

Editors

Nathalie Mornu

Kevin Kopp

Technical Editor

Melissa Grakowsky Shippee

Proofreader

Valerie Van Arsdale Shrader

Art Director

Carol Barnao

Production

Kay Holmes Stafford

Illustrator

Paulette Baron

Photographer

Carrie Johnson

Cover Designer

Carol Barnao

LARK JEWELRY & BEADING

An Imprint of Sterling Publishing
387 Park Avenue South
New York, NY 10016

ISBN 978-1-4547-0817-9

Library of Congress Cataloging-in-Publication Data

Katz, Amy.
  Seed bead chic : 25 elegant projects inspired by fine jewelry / Amy Katz.
    pages cm -- (Lark jewelry & beading bead inspirations)
  Summary: "Amy Katz teaches how to make seed bead jewelry projects resembling beautiful fine jewelry. Along with the stunning photography, step-by-step instructions, and beading diagrams, this book will introduce Amy's newly invented beading stitch: the right angle ladder stitch. This book will position primarily toward the dedicated intermediate to advanced audience"-- Provided by publisher.
  ISBN 978-1-4547-0817-9 (paperback)
  1. Beadwork--Patterns. 2. Jewelry making. I. Title.
  TT860.K38 2014
  745.594'2--dc23
                            2013047476

Distributed in Canada by Sterling Publishing
c/o Canadian Manda Group, 165 Dufferin Street
Toronto, Ontario, Canada M6K 3H6
Distributed in the United Kingdom by GMC Distribution Services
Castle Place, 166 High Street, Lewes, East Sussex, England BN7 1XU
Distributed in Australia by Capricorn Link (Australia) Pty. Ltd.
P.O. Box 704, Windsor, NSW 2756, Australia

For information about custom editions, special sales, and premium and corporate purchases, please contact Sterling Special Sales at 800-805-5489 or specialsales@sterlingpublishing.com.

Email academic@larkbooks.com for information about desk and examination copies. The complete policy can be found at larkcrafts.com.

Every effort has been made to ensure that all the information in this book is accurate. However, due to differing conditions, tools, and individual skills, the publisher cannot be responsible for any injuries, losses, and other damages that may result from the use of the information in this book.

Manufactured in China

2 4 6 8 10 9 7 5 3 1

larkcrafts.com

CONTENTS

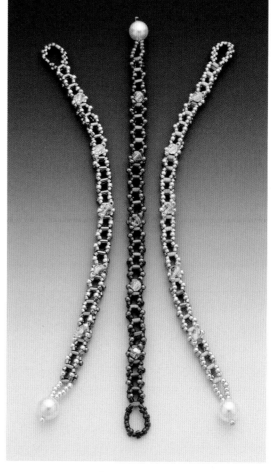

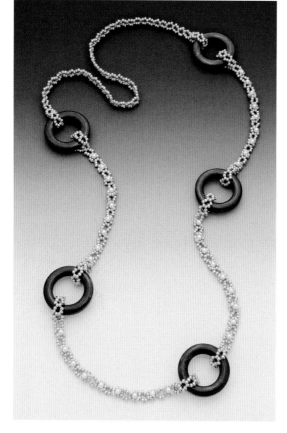

MATERIALS & TOOLS

Beaders love to incorporate many different types of materials into their work. While it is fun to have variety, the best advice I can offer is to purchase the highest quality materials you can afford for creating your pieces. Here are some of my suggestions for making your beadwork more pleasing.

Beads

Round Seed Beads

A palette of round seed beads in different sizes on a bead tray can inspire the creation of beautiful jewelry pieces. When using sizes 6°, 8°, 11°, and 15°, I prefer Japanese seed beads, hands down. While it seems logical that beads listed as the same size are uniform, don't be fooled. The sizes of beads vary slightly from manufacturer to manufacturer, as do shape and hole-size. Do your research and find the manufacturer that creates the bead that suites your need best.

In speaking about Japanese seed beads, I also have several other suggestions. In my experience, metallic beads hold shapes the best. Yes, I do use matte beads, glass beads, etc. in this book, but you will notice that all of the projects are metallic bead based. Many metallic beads are available in permanent finishes. Take advantage of this finish. If you are going to invest your time in a project, use top-quality seed beads.

In addition to Japanese round beads, I also praise the versatility of 15° Czech charlotte beads. Some of you may grimace at using such a small size, yet this bead does a magnificent finishing job. I suggest keeping these little wonders on hand. They are extremely useful for capturing and closing up areas that need to be pulled together to get the desired look.

Delicas

I recommend the brand Delica for several reasons, the main one being their size, which truly fits my comfort zone. Delica beads come in many colors, but two stand out above the rest: palladium-plated and gold-plated. I credit these beads with giving my pieces the fine-jewelry look I strive for. And while they do cost a little more than most cylinder beads, the result is unquestionably superior. Using Delicas will also give your pieces a rich look while you will sense a feeling of accomplishment just for incorporating them into your work.

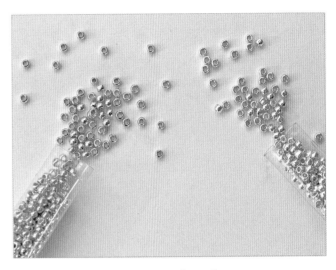

Round Seed Beads

Delicas

Bugle beads

Assorted crystals

Glass pearls

Bugle Beads

These are not your "grandmas beads" any longer. I love using size 1 bugles (very small) in my work. They are now available in many stunning colors that can add depth to your pieces.

A Word of Advice: While many artist will recommend that you purchase tons of different colored seed beads, my suggestion is a little different. Purchase the best gold, silver, bronze, and copper seed beads you can afford in as many shades as you can acquire. These shades will match your stones, crystals, and any other materials you typically would use in your work.

Crystals

Crystals are the soul of my jewelry pieces. They not only shine and sparkle, they add the finishing touches that produce a look of fine jewelry. I mainly use Swarovski crystals because quality matters. I insist on using the finest materials when I spend hours creating a piece. I am especially fond of the 2-mm round Swarovski crystals in color Crystal AB. Not only do these little wonders match everything, they add a subtle sparkle to each piece that very often fashions the perfect finishing touch. While 2-mm round crystals are a staple in my work, I also use a variety of different crystal shapes and sizes throughout the book.

Glass Pearls

Although I love the "real deal," glass pearls are uniform in shape and easy to use in projects. I primarily use Swarovski pearls because I like their finish and feel. I use pearls as accent beads as well as focal beads. While most of the pearls I use are round, glass pearls come in many shapes and sizes.

Thread

I have tried many threads throughout my years in the beading world. While none of them are perfect, I find the most pleasing to be FireLine. A spool of FireLine 6 lb. test can do the job for just about any project (although every once in a while I will use FireLine 4 lb. or FireLine 8 lb. test to meet the needs of a project). One disadvantage, however, with FireLine is the lack of rainbow colors available. If you really want to match your beads exactly, try coloring the FireLine with a permanent marker. In projects with numerous crystals, I can't imagine using any other thread, and it is much more sturdy than most threads.

Tools

Needles

My basic needle is a Size 12 Pony needle. When needles bend and break, I simply replace them with a new one. Sometimes I find a Size 13 English beading needle useful, especially when adding 15° charlottes to my work.

I have tried other needles as well. I like Tulip needles and find they are best used with large-holed seed beads. They resist bending, and can be used many times.

Scissors

My best advice is to use a sharp yet inexpensive pair of scissors. If you are cutting tons of FireLine, you will also be going through many scissors since that thread dulls the blade. There are also scissors available in fishing supply stores especially designed to cut fishing line. These specialized scissors can be a great tool as well.

Scissors

Beading Surfaces

I like using a surface that is portable and can be moved from room to room without having to transfer all of the beads. My favorite beading surface is Bead On It Boards. These boards come in a variety of shapes and sizes. Some are more portable for classroom work, and others are big enough to use as a lapboard.

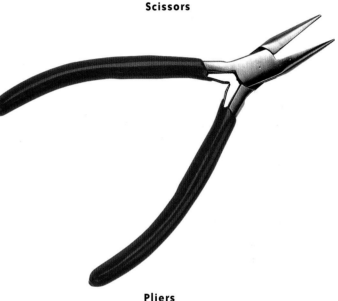

Pliers

I usually work with a pair of chain-nose pliers by my side. The reason being is I don't seem to be able to count. I always have an excess bead somewhere in the piece of jewelry. To get rid of it, I break the bead with my pliers, thus solving the issue without having to take out rows.

Pliers

Task Light

Illumination is really nice to help you see those tiny beads better. Task lights come in many sizes. At home, I use a large overhanging task light, and on the road, I take a portable one.

Triangle Tray

I find it easiest to scoop up the beads on my board with a triangle tray. I also use these trays when measuring bead grams on a scale.

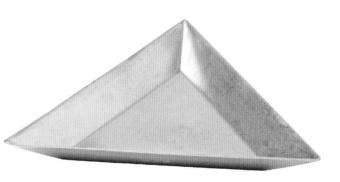

Triangle tray

Tape Measures

It is very useful to keep a tape measure on hand so you can size your jewelry properly.

Terminology

* Asterisks in Drawings

The asterisks indicate the start of a thread path.

FireLine

As stated, I use FireLine for my thread and suggest you do so as well. However, not everybody does, so I list FireLine in the Supply list for each project, but use the more generic word "thread" in the instructions, in case you choose a different thread.

Arm-Length of Thread

Though thread is normally measured in inches or centimeters, I decided to use the universal measurement of an arm-length. This is the distance from the tip of your longest finger to your shoulder. If you have short arms, add a little extra thread; people with long arms should use a bit less.

Wingspan

A wingspan is the length from the tip of your longest finger on one hand to the longest on your other hand when both arms are extended. Again, if you have short arms, add a little thread; people with longer arms should use a little bit less.

One Bead Down on the Diagonal (Peyote Stitch)

When completing the final row of peyote stitch, many of the projects will ask you to move the needle down one bead on the diagonal (into the second to last row). This stitch is a set-up for the process of stitching in the ditch.

Stitch in the Ditch (Even-count Peyote Stitch)

Once you have moved your needle one bead down on the diagonal, it will be positioned in between two stitches. Pick up a bead (or beads) as indicated, and sew through the next bead in the row (directly across). Follow the instructions and keep sewing across until filling the row with the desired beads. This technique can be used both for decorative purposes or to add a structure on top of a beaded element using even-count peyote stitch.

Ladder Up or Down

When beading in right angle ladder stitch, you are essentially building simultaneous units on upper and lower sides, one at a time. Once you have completed a unit, you will want to ladder up or ladder down, depending on where the needle needs to be positioned next. When laddering up or down, perform a ladder stitch without adding any beads.

Stopper Bead

A stopper bead is used to temporarily hold the project beads in place. Use a size 11° or larger bead that you can distinguish from the project beads and place it on the end of your thread. Run the needle through it on the opposite end to hold it there. String the indicated number of beads for the project. Once you have completed stitching one row, slide the stopper bead off the end.

"Up" Bead for Even-count Peyote Stitch

After completing the first row of even-count peyote stitch (actually, the first two rows make three rows), notice that the first bead is up, and the next is down. With the needle starting in the "up" bead, sew through to the next "up" bead (skipping the bead that is in the center of the two).

Project Levels and Difficulty

Each project in this book has been assigned a level: Beginner, All Levels, Intermediate, or Advanced. Beginner Projects are the most basic and good for people who are new to beading. All Level Projects are a bit more difficult than the basic project. These will be a challenge for a beginner and basic for anyone beyond the beginning level. Intermediate Projects are for beaders with a good understanding of most of the basic stitches. Various stitches may be mixed together in an intermediate project. Advanced Projects are for beaders familiar with many stitches and their complexities. The reader will have the ability to combine stitches and transition from stitch to stitch.

STITCHES & TECHNIQUES

Square Stitch

1 String a number of beads to complete the first row at your desired width, leaving a tail. Start a second row by adding one bead and circling back through the bead directly underneath, which would be the last bead in the first row (figure 1).

figure 1

2 String a second bead and continue threading through the bead directly underneath it (the second to last bead in the first row), and then again through the bead just added (figure 2).

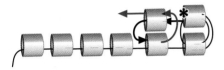

figure 2

3 Continue adding beads in this manner until reaching the end of the second row. Once completed, run the thread through the first and second rows of beads to reinforce it.

4 Continue the stitch row by row until reaching the desired length.

Even-Count Flat Peyote Stitch

1 String on a stopper bead and then pick up an even number of beads.

2 For the next row, pick up one bead and skip over the last bead in the previous row. Go through the next bead. Pick up one bead, skip over one bead, and go through the next bead. Continue stitching until reaching the end of the row (figure 3).

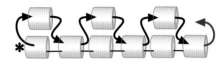

figure 3

Note: The first two rows of even-count flat peyote stitch make three rows.

3 To begin the next row and all subsequent rows, face the needle towards the beadwork. Pick up one bead and place it in the space at the beginning of the row. Pick up another bead, put the needle through the next "up" bead in the row (figure 4). Continue until reaching the end.

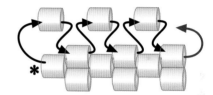

figure 4

Even-Count Tubular Peyote Stitch

1 String the indicated number of beads for the original row. Make sure the count is even. Create a ring by threading through the first three beads (figure 5).

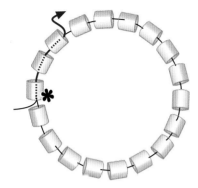

figure 5

2 Add an additional bead. Skip one bead on the row below (the original row) and go through the next bead in that row. Repeat until reaching the last stitch in the row (figure 6).

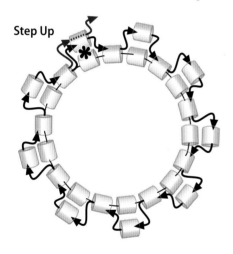

figure 6

3 Continue to follow figure 6. For the last stitch in the row, add one bead. Thread through the last bead of the original row and the first bead of the next row. The needle is now in place to start the next row.

Note: The first two rows of even-count tubular peyote stitch make three rows in total. From here on, you will be creating one row at a time.

Tubular Herringbone Stitch from a Brick Stitch Start

1 Pick up four beads. Sew through the first two beads, and then the third and fourth, to get them to stand side-by-side (figure 7). Pick up two more beads. Sew through the adjacent beads to create a third row.

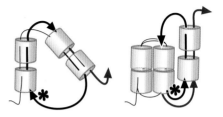

figure 7

2 Continue creating rows as indicated until reaching the desired length. Join the first and last rows by running the needle through the first. Reinforce all of the rows (figure 8).

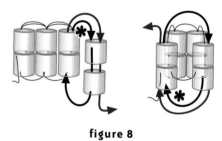

figure 8

3 Following figure 9 for steps 3, 4, and 5, exit from one row, pick up two beads and sew down through one bead in the next row. Stitch through the top bead in the next row.

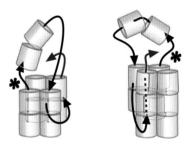

figure 9

4 Pick up two beads and again sew through one bead in the next row. Continue until reaching the last row.

5 For the last row, pick up two beads and sew through one bead in the next row. Sew through the top two beads in the next row to step up.

Right Angle Weave (RAW)

1 Pick up four beads and sew through all four again to create the first right angle weave square unit. Continue through the next two beads to position your needle for the next unit (figure 10).

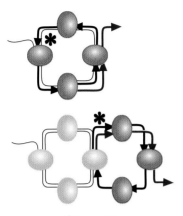

figure 10

2 Still following figure 10, pick up three beads and sew again through the bead on the side of the first unit. Continue through the next two beads of this second unit (where the needle should now be positioned on the side).

3 Continue repeating the stitch until reaching the desired length.

Add a Second Row

4 On the last unit in the first row, pass the needle through the next bead. This will position it in the second row (figure 11).

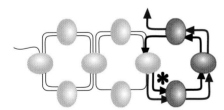

figure 11

5 Pick up three beads. Pass back through one bead on the existing unit, then through one bead in the next unit (figure 12).

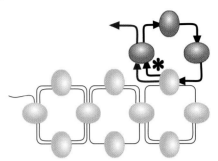

figure 12

6 For the next and all subsequent rows, the square unit already has two existing sides. Pick up two beads, run the needle through the bottom bead in the connecting unit in Row 1, the side bead of the last unit, the two beads just added, and the existing bead on the bottom of the next unit (figure 13).

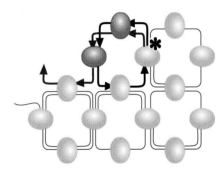

figure 13

7 Pick up two beads. Pass the needle through the bead on the side, the bead on the bottom, and the bead added on the last side of the new unit (figure 14).

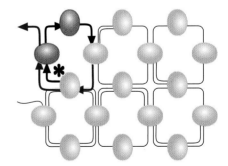

figure 14

8 Repeat the last two steps until reaching the end of the row.

Tubular Right Angle Weave

1 Pick up four beads. Move the needle over two additional beads to put it in place for the next RAW stitch. Then pick up three beads and do a RAW stitch (figure 10).

2 Pick up three more beads and do a RAW stitch. Move the needle to the top of the last square of RAW completed (figure 11).

3 Pick up three more beads and create one more right angle weave unit at the start of the second row (figure 12).

4 Stitch two more RAW units in row 2 (figures 13 and 14).

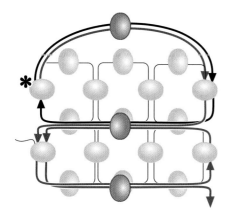

figure 15

Refer to figure 15 for steps 5 and 6.

5 Move the needle to the side of the last unit of RAW. Pick up one bead and sew through the side of the first RAW unit in row 2. Pick up one bead and sew through the side of the last RAW unit in row 2.

6 Move the needle through the top, the side, and the bottom of the third RAW unit in row 2, then the side of the first RAW unit in row 1. Pick up one bead and sew through the RAW in a square to close up the tube. This should result in a two-square tube of four RAW stitches total all the way around.

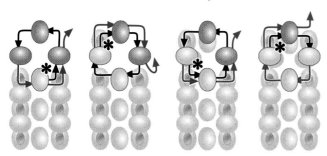

figure 16

Refer to figure 16 for steps 7 through 10.

7 Position the needle so it's exiting from one top bead in the tube. Pick up three beads and do a RAW stitch.

8 With the needle coming out of the side of the bead of the first added unit, pick up two beads and do one RAW stitch.

9 With the needle coming out of the top of the unit of the previous row, pick up two beads and do one RAW stitch.

10 With the needle coming out of the side of the previous RAW unit, pick up one bead. Put the needle through the side of the first RAW unit, then down through the top of the previous unit, through the side of the next unit, and finally through the top of the current unit.

11 Repeat the last four steps to make your tubular RAW as long as desired.

Right Angle Ladder Stitch

1 Pick up two bugle beads and ladder stitch once so they lie together side by side. Follow the tail in the drawings to orient your beadwork (figure 17).

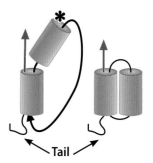

figure 17

2 Pick up one Delica, one 2-mm round crystal or other bead of a similar size, and one Delica. This will be known as Group 1. Pick up two bugle beads on the same thread. Ladder stitch them once so they lie together side by side (figure 18).

figure 18

3 With the needle coming out of the new bugle bead, pick up one Group 1. Stitch through the starting bugle bead on the opposite side to complete the front of the square (figure 19).

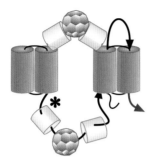

figure 19

4 Still following figure 19, ladder stitch down (ladder down) through the adjacent bugle beads without adding any beads.

5 With the needle now coming out of the back bugle bead, pick up one Delica, one 11° bead of a different color (or a bead of an equivalent size) and one Delica. This will be known as Group 2. Stitch through the next back bugle bead on the opposite side (figure 20).

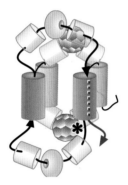

figure 20

6 Pick up one Group 2. Stitch through the next bugle to complete the unit.

7 Weave through the Group 2 beads and the next bugle. Ladder up without beads to the adjacent bugle in the front to position it for the next unit (figure 21).

figure 21

8 With the needle coming out of the front bugle bead, pick up one Group 1 and two bugles. Ladder stitch the bugle beads one time so they lay together side by side (figure 22).

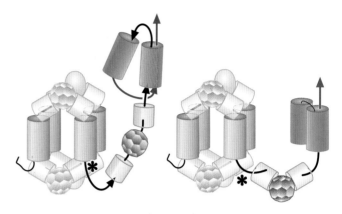

figure 22

9 Pick up one Group 1 and sew through the front bugle bead of the first unit. Ladder down through the adjacent bugle beads to the back (figure 23).

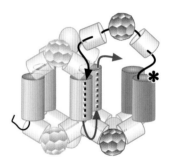

figure 23

10 Pick up one Group 2 and sew through the next back bugle. Pick up a second Group 2 and sew through the back bugle bead of unit 1 (figure 24).

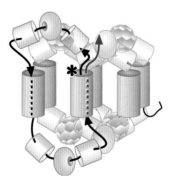

figure 24

11 Weave the needle through Group 2 and the next bugle bead. Ladder up through the adjacent bugle bead without adding any beads.

Fringe Stitch

1 With the needle coming out of one bead in the project, pick up additional beads in whatever order is indicated.

2 Put a small bead on the end as a stopper, after the last bead added.

3 Skip over the stopper and run the needle through all of the beads in the fringe.

4 Attach it through the indicted bead in the project.

Surrounding a Cabochon

1 Cut a piece of foundation approximately ½ inch (1.3 cm) larger than the stone's circumference. Glue the stone to the foundation. Let it dry for 20 minutes or longer.

2 Thread the needle and tie a thick knot at the end. Starting at the back of the foundation, pull the needle through so it is next to the stone. Pick up two beads and run the needle back through the foundation, then sew up through the foundation before the two beads, and again through the two beads just added (figure 25).

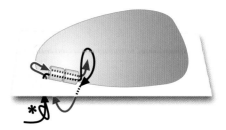

figure 25

3 Pick up two beads, and go back down through the foundation before sewing up through it again between the first and second bead added, then through the second bead added in the first stitch, as well as the two beads just added (figure 26). Repeat until there is an even number of beads around the stone.

figure 26

4 Do even-count tubular peyote stitch off the base just created until reaching the top of the stone (figure 27).

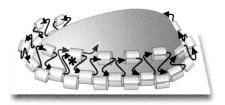

figure 27

Ending the Thread

Although I've tried just about every method, the best one for me is weaving and knotting. Once reaching the end of the thread, weave it circularly in and out of several beads. After a weave stitch or two, catch the weaving thread in between two beads. Create a loop around the beads and pull the needle through it to make a knot. Repeat at least three times to secure the work.

After the final knot, move the thread through several beads away from the knot. Cut the thread as close to the piece as possible or use a thread burner.

Opening and Closing a Jump Ring

Pick up two pairs of round-nose pliers and hold one in each hand. Use the pliers to open the jump ring by gently pulling one end of the ring towards you and gently pushing the other end away. Place the connecting element for your beaded item between the open ends of the jump ring. Reverse to gently position the ends back together and secure your item on the ring.

Making a Standard Clasp

Supplies
Size 11° seed beads, 1 g
Size 11° Delicas, 1 g
4 size 15° seed beads
7 round crystals, 2 mm
2 pearls, 3 mm
FireLine 6 lb. test

Stitches
Even-count flat peyote stitch, even-count tubular peyote stitch

The Toggle

1 Thread the needle with an arm-length of thread and leave a six-inch (15.2 cm) tail. String on 18 Delicas.

Note: Use a stopper bead at the end if helpful.

2 Do even-count flat peyote stitch for twelve rows. Remember, the first two rows make three rows.

3 Sew through the side of the peyote stitch to position the needle in the "up" bead of the first row.

4 Zip the first row and the last row together. Reinforce the last stitch several times (figure 28).

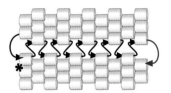

figure 28

5 With the needle coming out of the top of the peyote stitch, pick up one 15°, one 3-mm pearl, and one 15°. Put the needle through the opposite side of the top of the peyote stitch tube (figure 29).

figure 29

Note: Substitute bicones, round crystals, fire-polished, etc. for the 3-mm pearl as desired.

6 Weave the needle through the peyote stitch tube to the opposite end and repeat.

7 Weave in the thread, tie half-hitch knots, and end it.

The Ring

1 Thread the needle with one and one-half arm-lengths of thread and leave a six-inch (15.2 cm) tail. String on 28 Delicas and put the needle through the first three to make a ring.

2 Do even-count peyote stitch with Delicas for five rows. Remember the first two rows make three rows.

3 Weave in the tail, tie half-hitch knots, and end it.

4 Position the needle in between the first row of ditches at the very top. Pick up one 11° and put the needle through the adjacent Delica. Stitch in the ditches all the way around (figure 30).

figure 30

5 Once completed, move the needle down one Delica on the diagonal. Repeat this step (figure 31).

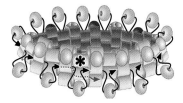

figure 31

6 Move the needle down one Delica on the diagonal. Tie a half-hitch knot. Stitch in the ditches all the way around with 2-mm round crystals. This will become the top of the clasp (figure 32).

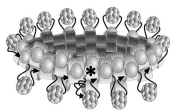

figure 32

7 Weave in the thread, tie half-hitch knots, and end it.

Note: Substitute 15°s, 11°s, and/or 2-mm round crystals in any way to stitch in the ditches.

earrings, rings, & brooch

SUPPLIES

Silver size 11° Delicas, 3-4 g

Gold size 15° seed beads, 1-2 g

1 stopper bead

FireLine 6 lb. test

Beading needles, size 12

DIMENSIONS

½ inch (1.3 cm) wide

STITCH

Even-count flat peyote stitch

LEVEL

Beginner

HIGH TENSION

Keep a nice, tight tension while doing the flat peyote stitch. While the ring won't be entirely stiff, you want it to fit as securely as possible.

SKY BAND RING

Big, bold jewelry is fun to wear but often time-consuming to create. Although I wouldn't give it up for the world, it's sometimes nice to bead something simple and fast. While sitting on a five-hour flight to a vacation destination, I decided to do just that. To keep myself amused, I made a strip of flat peyote, then stitched in some of the ditches for fun. This ring took less time than the flight, and I was able to wear it as I got off the plane.

1 Thread the needle with one and a half arm-lengths of thread. Leaving a 6-inch (15.2 cm) tail with a stop bead at the top of it, pick up 10 Delicas. Stitch even-count flat peyote using Delicas until you have a strip that's an even amount of rows and fits exactly around the finger.

Note: To get an even count, the first row of Delicas will have an "up" bead at one end. The last row of Delicas should have a "down" bead at the end to match the "up" bead on the other end. Add thread as necessary.

Embellish

2 With the needle coming out of the end Delica (facing side to side), sew it inward through the adjacent Delica on the side.

Turn the piece so it is facing up and down. Pick up one 15°. Stitch in the ditch (going upward). Stitch three more ditches with 15°s for a total of four rows of ditches (figure 1).

Note: You won't get to the very end because the last row is just a half ditch.

3 Still referring to figure 1, move the needle down through one Delica on the diagonal, then sew inward through the next adjacent Delica.

4 Repeat steps 2 and 3 until you've stitched in the ditch every third row with 15°s.

Zip

5 Position the needle so it's exiting from the end (first added) Delica bead in row 2.

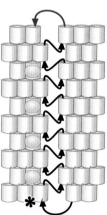

figure 2

6 Stitch across to the "up" bead in the last row, then stitch across to the "down" Delica bead in the first row. Repeat until all the Delicas are zipped together (figure 2). When you reach the last bead, reinforce the stitching several times. Depending on your bead count, you may need to add an additional embellishment row with 15°s along the zip. Weave in the thread, tie half-hitch knots, and end it.

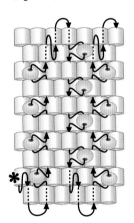

figure 1

> ### MIX IT UP
> Instead of embellishing the ring with 15° seed beads, try substituting 2-mm round crystals to give the band a sparkling look.

SUPPLIES

Copper gold metallic iris size 11° seed beads, 2 g

Gold-plated size 11° Delicas, 2 g

12 gold size 15° seed beads

2 vitrail medium round crystals, 10 mm

26 crystal AB round crystals, 2 mm

2¼ inches (5.7 cm) of fine gold chain

2 gold-colored jump rings, 6 mm

1 pair of gold ear wires

FireLine 6 lb. test

Beading needles, size 12

2 pair of needle-nose pliers

DIMENSIONS

2¾ inches (7 cm) long

STITCH

Even-count tubular peyote stitch

LEVEL

All Levels

SAME LENGTH

To make the earrings in matching lengths, you need to cut two identical pieces of chain. Here's how: String the top loop of each chain onto a beading needle. Make sure the needle is perfectly horizontal, then check that both pieces of chain are the same length.

DAZZLING DROP EARRINGS

Like anyone else, I love big, exuberant adornments covered with glitz. But it doesn't always require a lot of embellishment to highlight the beautiful beads in a piece of jewelry. I think the real trick behind designing is making the simplicity stand out. This sleek design will add a little sparkle to a night out. Best of all, you get a dazzling result with only a short investment of time spent beading!

Beaded Drop

1 Thread the needle with one and a half arm-lengths of thread. Leaving a 10-inch (25.4 cm) tail, pick up 26 Delicas and run the needle through the first three to make a ring.

2 Stitch in even-count tubular peyote for five rows, stepping up at the end of each row. (Remember, the first two rows make three rows.) Leave the needle in place.

3 Thread the tail, move it to the center of the peyote stitch, and pierce it through the inside of the ring. Pick up one 10-mm crystal. Pierce the needle through the opposite side of the peyote stitch in the circle. Reinforce it. Weave in the tail, tie half-hitch knots, and end it (figure 1).

figure 1

4 Go back to the working thread. Move the needle down one Delica bead on the diagonal in the base. Tie a half-hitch knot. Stitch in the first ditch with one 2-mm crystal. Continue stitching in each ditch with one 2-mm crystal until the row is complete (figure 2).

figure 2

5 Move the needle down one Delica on the diagonal in the base. Stitch in all the ditches in the row with one 11°. Repeat this step one more time to complete the final row. Weave in the thread, tie half-hitch knots, and cut the thread.

Finish

6 Position the needle so it's exiting from the middle row of ditches, from an 11° on one of the drops.

Note: Orient the hole in the 10-mm crystal either perfectly horizontal or vertical. Because the hole will be somewhat visible in the finished piece, you want it positioned in a visually pleasing way.

7 Cut the chain into two 1-inch (2.5 cm) pieces and set one aside for when you make the second earring. Pick up three 15°s, the piece of chain, and three 15°s. Put the needle back through the 11° on the base and through all the beads and chain to reinforce. Weave in the thread, tie half-hitch knots, and end it (figure 3).

figure 3

8 Open one jump ring with the needle-nose pliers. Place the chain and an ear wire in the jump ring, then close it.

Repeat all steps to make a second earring.

endless earrings

Most beaders favor certain color palettes, and many of us gravitate towards creating certain shapes. For example, this book contains many circular or ring-shaped components within each final creation. Having this fascination with circular pieces, I couldn't think of anything more "me" than a hoop earring.

The most difficult part of planning this earring was deciding how large to make the hoop. While I like having some presence, I don't want it to be overbearing. And so I went for a medium-sized piece. I decided to make a small "holder" for the hoop in a contrasting color because it adds a unique touch and a timeless style.

SUPPLIES

Gun metal size 11° seed beads, 1.5 g (color A)

Silver size 11° seed beads, 1.5 g (color B)

Silver size 11° Delicas, 2.6 g (color C)

Black size 11° Delicas, 0.5 g (color D)

16 silver size 15° seed beads

30 crystal AB round crystals, 2 mm

1 pair of ear wires

FireLine 6 lb. test

Beading needle, size 12

STITCHES

Even-count tubular peyote stitch

Even-count flat peyote stitch

LEVEL

All Levels

HALF THE NUMBER OF DITCHES

This tip involves a little math (my apologies in advance). If you decide to do a hoop that is 60 Delicas around, you will have 30 ditches (always half the amount of ditches to Delicas). This will make for a one-to-one placement of crystals and 11° seed beads. However, if you prefer your hoop to be 70 Delicas around, you will have 35 ditches. When you stitch in the ditches alternating crystals and seed beads, your last stitch will either have two crystals or two 11° beads next to each other. In other words, if you want the crystals and seed beads distributed evenly in each ditch, choose an amount of Delicas in your hoop that divides by four.

Make the Hoop

1 Thread a needle with one and a half arm-lengths of thread, leaving a 6-inch (15.2 cm) tail. String 60 C beads and thread the needle through the first three to make a ring.

2 Do even-count tubular peyote stitch for five rows. (Remember, the first two rows of this stitch make three rows. From here on, you will be creating one row at a time.) Step up at the end of each row.

3 As illustrated in figure 1, move the needle down one C on the diagonal. Tie a half-hitch knot. Stitch in each ditch, alternating one A and one 2-mm crystal all the way around until reaching the end of the row. Following the red thread path, next move the needle down one C on the diagonal as shown in figure 1.

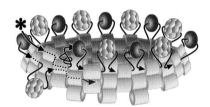

figure 1

4 Stitch in each ditch in the row with one B (figure 2).

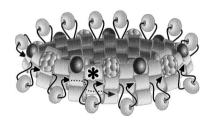

figure 2

MIX IT UP

Don't be afraid to make your hoop larger or smaller depending upon the look you wish to achieve. It will work as long as the piece is done using an even number of Delica beads. Keep in mind that really large hoops will be more floppy than smaller ones.

5 Again move the needle down one C on the diagonal. Stitch in each ditch in the row with one A (figure 3).

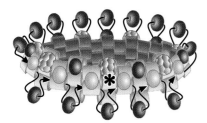

figure 3

6 Weave in the tail, tie half-hitch knots, and end it.

Create the Band

7 Thread the needle with one and a half arm-lengths of Fire Line, leaving a 6-inch (15.2 cm) tail. String a stopper bead on the end. Pick up eight D beads.

8 Stitch even-count flat peyote for 34 rows with the D beads. Remove the stopper bead after completing the first row.

9 Weave in the tail, tie half-hitch knots, and end it.

10 Place the band around the hoop. Zip the ends of the band together so that it serves as a bail for the hoop as illustrated in the lower half of figure 4 (figure 4).

figure 4

11 Thread the needle through one of the D beads near the middle of the band. Pick up four 15°s, one ear wire (connected so the crystals in the hoop face the front), and four more 15°s. Sew back through the D where you started this step, as well as through the four 15°s, the ear wire, and the four 15°s to reinforce.

12 Weave in the thread, tie half-hitch knots, and end it.

Repeat all steps to make a second earring.

SUPPLIES

Silver size 11° Delicas, 4 g (color A)

Black size 11° Delicas, 2.5 g (color B)

Silver size 15° seed beads, 1 g

1 crystal AB round crystal, 8 mm

28 crystal AB round crystals, 2 mm

1 silver pin back, ¾ inch (1.9 cm)

FireLine 6 lb. test

Beading needles, size 12

DIMENSIONS

1¼ x 1⅝ inches (3.2 x 4.1 cm)

STITCH

Square stitch

LEVEL

Intermediate

START TIGHT

To make square stitch sturdier at the start, after completing the first two rows, run the thread back through both rows. This will tighten it and make it easier to work with in subsequent rows.

art deco brooch

"I had a happy accident." Beaders often use this phrase! That's exactly what happened with this piece. I started with one idea that turned into something completely different. Originally, I wanted to create a pendant using square stitch that was flat, square, and accented with crystals. During the process of designing it, I began to bend it and twist it into different shapes. I do this whenever I create; it gives me a different perspective. In bending the square stitch and sewing it together in a unique way, I discovered a great brooch.

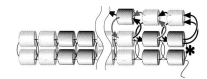

MIX IT UP

Patterns in square stitch are simple to follow, allowing you to alter the design to your heart's content. If you don't care for checkers, why not try a striped pattern? The inside piece, which I beaded in one color, can also be made in a pattern that complements the outside. And if you don't like patterns at all, create the piece in two solid colors. Pearls and even small gemstones can act as the fringe and/or the focal bead. The fringe can also be made longer by adding additional 15°s.

Make this piece uniquely yours by spending time playing with the fold and deciding how you'd like to attach it together. The fold is the key to giving the brooch your own special trademark. And if you like the concept but would like a bigger piece, try adding additional square stitch rows. Be sure to note the number of rows so you make both pieces the same length.

3 In the next row, reverse the pattern by square stitching Bs over the As of the previous row, and As over Bs of the previous row (figure 2).

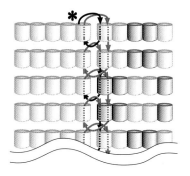

figure 2

4 In the next row, square stitch Bs over Bs of the previous row, and As over As of the previous row.

5 Adding thread as necessary, repeat steps 3 and 4, reversing the pattern every two rows, until you have 16 rows total. Weave in the tail, tie half-hitch knots, and end it. Leave the working thread in place.

6 Begin a second piece by threading the needle onto one wingspan of thread and leaving a 6-inch (15.2 cm) tail. Pick up 20 As. Bead 16 rows of square stitch with As. Weave in the tail, tie half-hitch knots, and end it. Leave the working thread in place.

Attach the Pieces

7 Place the first piece down onto the second piece so the beads are oriented in the same direction. If one of the working threads is long enough, weave it to one end where the Delicas in the end rows of both pieces line up; otherwise, add thread. Square stitch the end rows of the pieces together without adding any beads (figure 3). Repeat on the other end.

figure 3

8 Move the needle to the nearest edge of one piece where the Delicas face the other way. Bring your needle out of the first Delica on the patterned side.

Brooch Base

1 Thread the needle with one wingspan of thread. Leaving a 6-inch (15.2 cm) tail, pick up two As and two Bs. Repeat five times to string on 20 Delicas total.

2 For the next row, square stitch As over the As of the previous row, and Bs over the Bs of the previous row (figure 1).

figure 1

9 Pick up one 15°, one B, and one 2-mm crystal. Put the needle back through the B. Pick up one 15° and put the needle through the adjacent A in the non-patterned side. Move the needle through the next A in the non-patterned side so it is facing upward. Pick up one 15°, one B, and one 2-mm crystal. Put the needle back through the B. Pick up one 15° and put the needle through the adjacent Delica in the patterned side (figure 4).

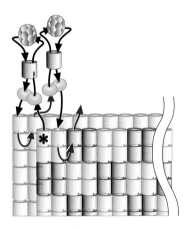

figure 4

10 Repeat step 9 until all the edge beads have a fringe. Then repeat step 9 on the opposite edge. Leave the thread in place.

Fold

Refer to figure 5 for the remaining steps.

11 This is where your creativity comes into play. Fold the piece in a pleasing way. Once you're happy with the result, make the fold permanent by tacking down a few of the Delicas on the end of the top of the piece to the Delicas on the end of the bottom of the piece.

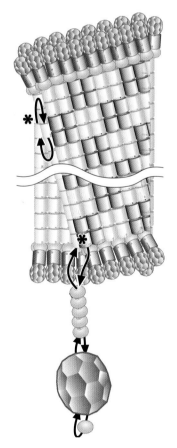

figure 5

12 Decide where you'd like to dangle the large crystal. Still referring to figure 5, position the needle at that spot and pick up five 15°s, the 8-mm crystal, and one 15°. Put the needle back through the crystal and the five 15°s. Weave in the thread, tie half-hitch knots, and end it.

13 Thread the needle with 18 inches (45.7 cm) of thread and weave it into the back of the piece. Sew on the pin back, reinforcing it several times. Weave in the thread, tie half-hitch knots, and end it.

Beautifully Bold Ring

Many of us purchase beautiful cabochons without ever knowing what we're going to do to showcase them to their fullest—I'm totally guilty of this. Here's a great idea for that one standout stone. I came across a beautiful piece of labradorite at a bead show, and knew right then and there that it would become a ring.

I'm usually guided by my idea for a design rather than by a particular focal element. In this case, however, the shape of the stone drove the design itself. This is a little different approach for me, and I always like to expand the way I think about making jewelry.

SUPPLIES

Silver size 11° seed beads, 1 g

Silver size 11° Delica beads, 3 g

Silver size 15° seed beads, 2 g

40 crystal AB round crystals, 2 mm

1 triangular stone cabochon,
34 x 18 mm

1³⁄₄ x 1¹⁄₄ inches (4.4 x 3.2 cm)
of beading foundation*

1³⁄₄ x 1¹⁄₄ inches (4.4 x 3.2 cm)
of synthetic suede*

Jewelry glue

FireLine 6 lb. test

Beading needles, size 12

* If your focal element is a different size
than the one pictured, get a piece of
foundation/suede about ¹⁄₂ inch (1.3 cm)
larger than the diameter of your rivoli or
cabochon.

DIMENSIONS

Size variable

STITCHES

Even-count tubular peyote stitch

Bead embroidery

LEVEL

Intermediate

MIX IT UP

Almost no two cabochons are
exactly alike, and that's the beauty
of working with stones. Find one
that best suits your personality
based on color, size, or shape,
and then create this piece around
it. Do you like bright shades, or
stones that are more demur in
color? Do you want something
more faceted, or shapely and
smooth? Big and bold works better
for some people and smaller and
more delicate for others. In other
words, follow the rough idea of
my instructions, but give the piece
your own personal trademark.

Create the Band

1 Thread the needle with one wingspan
of thread and leave a 6-inch (15.2 cm)
tail. Pick up an even number of Delicas
that fit approximately two beads larger
than the width of your finger (if you're
a tight beader, use four beads). Put the
needle through the first three beads to
create a circle.

2 Stitch in even-count tubular peyote
with Delicas for 15 rows (don't forget
that the first two rows make three rows,
and remember to step up at the end of
each row). Once completed, weave in
the tail, tie half-hitch knots, and end it.
Leave the working thread in place.

Bezel the Stone

3 Glue the stone to the center of
the beading foundation. Let it dry
for at least 20 minutes. Do not cut
the foundation!

4 Thread the needle with one and a half
arm-lengths of thread, and tie a thick
knot at the end. Working from the back
of the beading foundation, push the
needle through so it's next to the stone.

5 Pick up two Delicas, run the needle back
through the beading foundation, then
sew up through the foundation again and
through the two Delicas (figure 1).

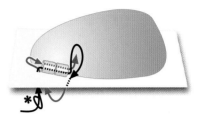

figure 1

6 Pick up two Delicas, take the needle
back through the beading foundation,
then sew up through the foundation
and the last Delica added in the first
stitch plus the two Delicas just added
(figure 2).

figure 2

7 Repeat step 6 until an even count of
Delicas surrounds the stone. Stitch in
even-count tubular peyote for four to
seven rows (depending on the depth of
the stone), as shown in figure 3.

figure 3

When you reach just the top of the stone, stitch one final row of even-count tubular peyote stitch using 15°s (figure 4).

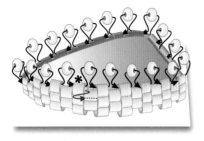

figure 4

Note: If you need to make the bezel tighter around the top of the stone, you can also add a row of 15° Czech Charlottes as an option.

Variation

8 Move the needle down one Delica bead on the diagonal and tie a half-hitch knot. Stitch in the ditch all the way around, alternating one 11° seed bead and one 2-mm round crystal. Once completed, weave the thread through the foundation, knot it, and end it (figure 5).

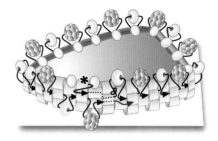

figure 5

9 Cut the beading foundation close to the edge of the stone, leaving about 1/16 inch (1.6 mm) all around. Glue the beading foundation to the synthetic suede. Let it dry for at least 20 minutes. Cut the synthetic suede to fit the dimensions of the stone.

10 Thread the needle with one arm-length of thread, and tie a knot at the end. Push the needle in between the synthetic suede and the beading foundation and up through the foundation. Pick up one 15°, one 2-mm round crystal, and one 15°. Sew through the foundation, the synthetic suede, and the last 15° added (figure 6).

figure 6

11 Pick up one 11° seed bead and one 15°. Sew through the synthetic suede, the foundation, and the last 15° added. Pick up one 15° and one 2-mm round crystal. Sew through the synthetic suede, the foundation, and the last 15° added, making a picot (figure 7).

figure 7

12 Repeat step 11 until you've added picots all around the bottom of the stone.

Note: For the last picot, pick up one 2-mm round and sew the first and last stitches together using the 15° from each as a base. Once completed, weave in the thread to through the foundation, tie knots, and end it.

Attach the Stone to the Band

13 Weave the needle to one end of the band (through and up a Delica). Sew through the synthetic suede and into the next Delica. Repeat until the entire stone is attached on one side (figure 8).

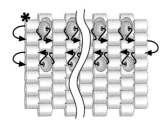

figure 8

14 Repeat step 13 on the opposite end of the stone.

Finish the Band

15 Use an existing thread or thread the needle with one and a half arm-lengths of thread. Leaving a 6-inch (15.2 cm) tail, position the needle so it's coming out of the second row of Delicas closest to the stone.

16 Pick up one 15° and stitch in the ditch. Continue stitching the ditch until you reach the stone on the other side of the band (figure 8).

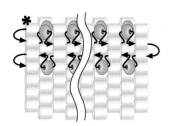

figure 8

17 Turn the needle around by putting it through the adjacent Delica. Then repeat step 16.

18 Repeat steps 16 and 17 until all the ditches in the band are stitched. Weave in the tail, tie half-hitch knots, and end it.

Finish Attaching the Stone

19 Position the needle so it's in the 15° closest to a side where the stone is attached. Whipstitch the 15° to the picot in the bottom fringe of the ring. Continue whipstitching until the 15°s and picots on the side of the stone are all attached. Weave in the thread, tie half-hitch knots, and end it (figure 9).

figure 9

20 Thread the needle with 12 inches (30.5 cm) of thread, and weave it into the opposite side of the band next to the stone. Repeat step 19. Weave in the thread, tie half-hitch knots, and end it.

SUPPLIES

Silver size 11° seed beads, 2 g

Silver size 11° Delicas, 2 g

Silver size 15° seed beads, 1.5 g

2 aquamarine crystals, 8 mm

2 white crystal pearls, 6 mm

10 white crystal pearls, 3 mm

10 crystal AB round crystals, 2 mm

2 crystal AB crystal briolettes,
11 x 5.5 m

1 pair of silver ear wires

FireLine 6 lb. test

Beading needles, size 12

DIMENSIONS

2¼ inches (5.7 cm)

STITCH

Even-count tubular peyote

Fringe stitch

LEVEL

Intermediate

WHY STITCH IN THE DITCH?

Stitching in the ditches does several things to enhance the piece and make it more wearable. It stiffens the peyote stitch, providing a more solid base. It also provides another row off of the peyote stitch to add things like fringe or to attach components together.

PERFECT TOUCH earrings

I love earrings that have some presence but don't take over. This pair is showy enough to add elegance to an outfit, but they're not overbearing. The earrings look as good with jeans as they do with elegant evening wear. I like my earrings to be versatile!

One of my favorite things to do when beading is even-count tubular peyote stitch and then fill in the ditches with beads. I guess everyone has an obsession, and this is mine. These earrings are chock full of my favorite stitch.

Bottom Component

1 Thread the needle with one arm length of thread. Leaving an 8-inch (20.3 cm) tail, pick up 22 Delicas and put the needle through the first three strung to make a ring. Stitch even-count tubular peyote for five rows. Remember, the first two rows of peyote stitch make three rows.

2 Move the needle through the Delicas to the middle of the piece. Pierce the needle through to the inside of the piece. Pick up one 8-mm pearl. Sew through the pearl and then through one Delica in the middle row straight across from where the thread exited on the other side. Go back through the pearl and then the Delica originally exited. Reinforce it again.

3 Move the needle to the top "up" Delicas. Stitch one row of even-count tubular peyote stitch using 15°s (figure 1).

figure 1

4 Still referring to figure 1, move the needle down two Delicas on the diagonal. Stitch in the ditches with 11°s all the way around. Leave the thread in place.

5 Thread the tail. Make sure the thread is coming out of an "up" Delica. Stitch one row of even-count tubular peyote with 15°s (figure 2). Weave in the tail, tie half-hitch knots, and end it.

figure 2

Top Component

6 Thread the needle with one and a half arm-lengths of thread. Leaving a 6-inch (15.2 cm) tail, pick up 20 Delicas and put the needle through the first three to make a ring. Stitch five rows of even-count tubular peyote. (Remember the first two rows make three rows.) Step up at the end of each row. Weave in the tail, tie half-hitch knots, and end it.

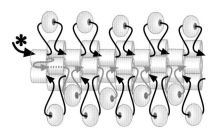

figure 3

7 Weave the needle to the top row of ditches. Stitch in the ditch with 11°s (figure 3).

Note: Figure 3 is shown flat for easy viewing.

8 Still referring to figure 3, move the needle down one Delica on the diagonal in the base. Stitch in the ditch with 11°s. Repeat.

Variation

9 Weave the needle through an 11° on the top row of ditches. Begin the fringe stitch by picking up two 15°s, one 3-mm pearl, and one 15°. Put the needle back through the pearl. Pick up two 15°s. Sew through the next 11° in the row. Pick up two 15°s, one 2-mm round, and one 15°. Put the needle back through the 2-mm round. Pick up two 15°s. Sew through the next 11° in the row. Repeat the pattern all the way around (figure 4). Leave the remaining thread in place (figure 4).

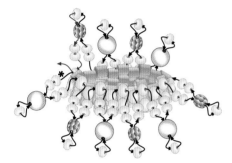

figure 4

Assembly

10 Thread the needle onto the excess thread of the bottom component and position the needle so it's exiting from an 11° in the ditch. Pick up three 11°s, a briolette, and three 11°s. Put the needle back through the adjacent 11° in the ditch to attach, forming a circle. Reinforce once (figure 5).

figure 5

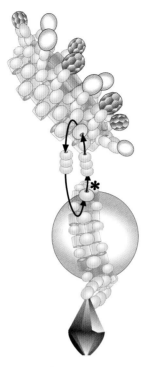

figure 6

11 Weave the thread up through the Delicas on the bottom component to an 11° on the opposite side. Pick up three 11°s and put the needle through an 11° in the middle row of the top component located directly underneath a 2-mm round fringe. Pick up three 11°s and put the needle back through the same 11° on the bottom component. Reinforce once (figure 6). Weave in the thread, tie half-hitch knots, and end it.

12 Thread the needle onto the excess thread of the top component. Weave the needle through the Delicas and position it so it's in a middle 11° in the ditch underneath a pearl fringe.

Note: Make sure the top component is perfectly centered over the bottom one.

13 Pick up four 15°s, an earring finding, and four 15°s. Put the needle back through the original 11° in the top component. Reinforce once. Move the needle through the Delicas to the side of the circle. Position the needle so it's exiting from a top "up" Delica in the ring. Pick up an 8-mm round crystal. Put the needle through an "up" Delica on the opposite side of the ring, sewing through on the opposite end. Put the needle back through the 8-mm round crystal and the first "up" Delica to reinforce (figure 7).

Note: The hole in the crystal should be horizontal.

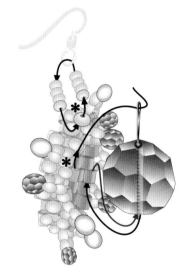

figure 7

14 Weave in the thread, tie half-hitch knots, and end it.

Repeat all steps to make a second earring.

SUPPLIES

Gold size 11° Delicas, 3 g

Gold size 15° seed beads, 1 g

2 crystal AB rondelle crystals,
6 x 8 mm

6 fuchsia round crystals, 4 mm

50 crystal AB round crystals, 2 mm

1 pair of gold ear wires

FireLine 6 lb. test

Beading needles, size 12

DIMENSIONS

2³⁄₈ inches (6 cm) long

STITCHES

Square stitch

Tubular even-count peyote stitch

LEVEL

Advanced

SQUARE STITCH VS. LADDER STITCH

Square stitch is sturdier because it has more thread paths than ladder stitch, and that's why I chose it for these earrings. When attaching the crystals, you want a piece that is tightly stitched together and won't separate, leaving unwanted spaces. Square stitch also allows you to run the needle between the two stitches with no problem so you can easily pierce between the two Delicas and then put the thread through the crystals to attach them.

CITY LIGHTS earrings

These earrings add a real splash of color to any outfit. I really love the challenge of their design. It does take some skill to make them since the placement of the crystals at the center isn't done by an exact formula. As you create them, you will realize that the components have many other design possibilities. I made a necklace based on this design that was a 2010 Fire Mountain Gems Finalist.

Square-Stitch Connectors

Connector 1

1 Thread the needle with one and a half arm-lengths of thread. Leaving a 6-inch (15.2 cm) tail with a stopper bead on it, string on 30 Delicas.

2 Square stitch for one row, then reinforce it by running the needle once through the first and second rows. Remove the stopper bead. Weave in the tail, tie half-hitch knots, and end it. Leave the working thread in place.

Connector 2

3 Thread the needle with one arm-length of thread. Leaving a 6-inch (15.2 cm) tail with a stopper bead on it, string on 18 Delicas. Repeat step 2.

Circle Components

4 Thread the needle with one arm-length of thread. Leaving a 6-inch (15.2 cm) tail, string on 16 Delicas and go through the first three to make a ring.

5 Stitch even-count peyote for five rows (remember, the first two rows make three rows). Remember to step up at the end of each row.

6 Move the needle down one Delica on the diagonal in the base. Stitch in each ditch with one 15° all the way around.

7 Move the needle down one Delica on the diagonal in the base. Tie a half-hitch knot. Stitch in each ditch with one 2-mm round crystal all the way around.

8 Repeat step 6.

9 Make two more circles, for a total of three, by repeating steps 4 to 8. For two of them, weave in the threads, tie half-hitch knots, and end it. On the remaining one, weave in the tail, tie-half hitch knots, and end it, but leave the working thread in place.

Connect the Components

10 String Connector 1 through the two circle components that have no working threads. Form it into a ring by connecting the ends with a square stitch without adding any beads. Reinforce it several times. Run the needle through a few rows of square stitch on either side to reinforce it even more (figure 1).

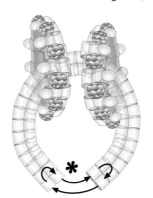

figure 1

11 Pierce the needle inwards inside the square stitch strip (between the threads in between the two rows of Delicas.). Line up the circle components on either side of Connector 1. Position your needle next to one of the circles as closely as possible.

12 Pick up one 4-mm crystal. Put the needle through the crystal, and go through the middle of the square stitch row directly above the crystal on the opposite side (between the two rows). Exit out of one the Delicas, then run the needle through three rows of Delicas (figure 2).

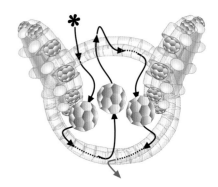

figure 2

13 Repeat step 12 twice to add two more 4-mm crystals. Leave the working thread in place. This piece of beadwork will now be called the centerpiece.

14 Pass Connector 2 through the two circle components and close it into a ring as described in step 10. This will be the top of the earring. Center the needle between two Delicas in the middle of Connector 2. String on four 15°s, one ear wire, and four 15°s (figure 3). Weave through the 15°s and the ear wire several times to secure. Weave the thread through the square stitch, tie half-hitch knots, and end it.

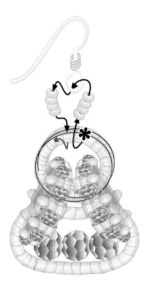

figure 3

15 Go back to the working thread in the centerpiece. Position it so that it is two rows of square stitch away from the center 4-mm round crystal on one side.

16 Now you'll attach the bottom-most circle component to the centerpiece. String on eleven Delicas. Pick up the remaining circle component and string it on the Delicas. Count four rows of square stitch from the starting point and put the needle through it to attach. Secure the thread, then weave it in, tie half-hitch knots, and end it.

Variation

Decorative Drop

17 Using the remaining working thread on the bottom-most circle component, position it through one 2-mm round in the ditch. Pick up three 15°s, one crystal rondelle, and one 2-mm round crystal. Put the needle back through the crystal rondelle and the three 15°s. Put the needle through the original 2-mm round crystal in the circle ditch. Weave in the thread, tie half-hitch knots, and end it.

Repeat all steps to make a second earring.

LI'L SPARKLE EARRINGS

Right angle ladder stitch is a one that I had created but not fully explored. For instance, I had never tried making earrings using the stitch until this pair. I thought long and hard about how to get a result that sparkles, and this design didn't take off until I rotated the square units diagonally. As a result, these diamond-shaped earrings covered with crystals and pearls can be created in many color combinations with endless embellishment possibilities.

Unit One

1 The earring's centerpiece diamond shape consists of four units, each with a front and a back side. To begin, thread the needle with one and a half arm-lengths of thread, leaving a six-inch (15.2 cm) tail. Pick up two bugle beads and ladder stitch them together so they lie side by side (figure 1).

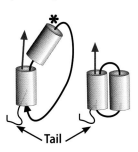

figure 1

2 Pick up one Delica bead, one A, and one Delica (this pattern will be called Group 1). Using the same thread, pick up two more bugles and ladder stitch them together so they lie side by side figure 2.

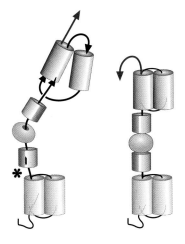

figure 2

3 Pick up a second Group 1. Stitch through the corresponding bugle on the opposite side as illustrated in figure 3 to complete the bottom of the first square unit. Ladder down through the adjacent bugle without adding any beads (figure 3).

figure 3

4 Now work on the back of the unit. Pick up one Delica, one B, and one Delica (this pattern will be called Group 2). Following figure 4 (left), stitch through the next back bugle on the opposite side where the thread is coming out. Pick up another Group 2. Repeat to complete the back of the unit (figure 4).

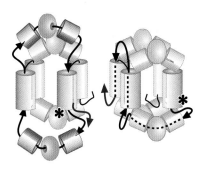

figure 4

5 Following figure 4 (right), sew through the first Group 2 and the next bugle, and ladder down to the next bugle without adding any beads.

Unit Two

6 Flip the beadwork over to return to the front side, working on the second unit. With the needle coming out of the front bugle, pick up one Group 1 and two bugles. Ladder stitch the bugles together one time so they lie side by side (figure 5).

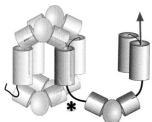

figure 5

7 Pick up one Group 1 and sew through the front bugle of the first unit. Ladder through the adjacent bugle to the back without adding any beads (figure 6).

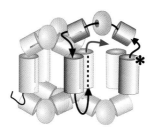

figure 6

8 Returning to the work on the back side of unit 2, pick up one Group 2 and sew through the next bugle. Pick up another Group 2 and sew through the first bugle (figure 7). Upon exiting, follow figure 8 and sew again through the Group 2 and the next bugle, and ladder through the adjacent bugle without adding any beads.

figure 7

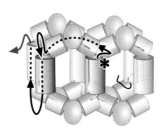

figure 8

Unit Three

9 Flip the beadwork over. Working on the front side again, now start the third unit, sewing through one Group 1 as illustrated in figure 9. Pick up two bugles and ladder stitch together.

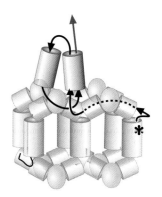

figure 9

10 Pick up a Group 1 followed by two bugles and ladder stitch the bugles together (figure 10).

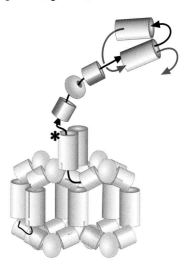

figure 10

Front (left) and back (right)

13 To start the front side of the fourth (last) unit, pick up a Group 1 followed by two bugles (figure 13). Ladder stitch the two bugles together. Sew through the Group 1 and the next bugle. Then ladder up through the adjacent bugle to the back.

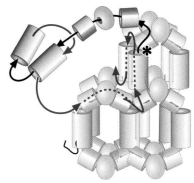

figure 13

14 Once again flip the beadwork over to work on the back layer. Sew through the Group 2. Sew up to the top bugle, pick up a Group 2, and sew down through the next bugle. Then, sew again through the same Group 2 and bugle as before, and ladder down through the adjacent bugle to the back (figure 14).

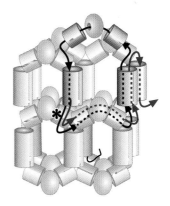

figure 14

11 Following figure 11, sew through the closest Group 1, then the next bugle. Ladder down through the adjacent bugle without adding any beads.

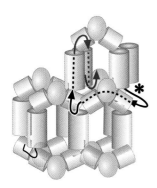

figure 11

12 To work on the back side of this unit, flip the beadwork over and sew through the Group 2 and bugle as illustrated in figure 12. Pick up a Group 2 and sew down through the bugle. Ladder up through the adjacent bugle to the back.

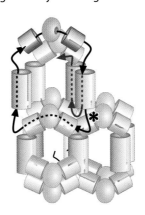

figure 12

Embellishing the Focal Diamond

15 Position the needle so it is coming out of the top of the bugle, pick up one 15°, one 3-mm round crystal, and one 15°. Sew into the next bugle as shown in figure 15, so that the round crystal sits in the middle of the unit.

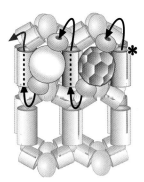

figure 15

Still following figure 15, pick up one 15°, one 3-mm pearl, and one 15°. Sew into the next bugle in the opposite way so the 3-mm pearl sits in the middle of the adjacent unit.

16 Weave the needle to the outside of the next unit. Repeat step 15. Once completed, leave the needle positioned between the bugle and the Delica in the last stitch (figure 16).

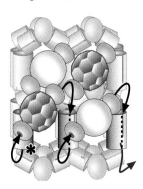

figure 16

17 With the needle coming out of the bugle as shown in the bottom portion of figure 17, string three 15°s, one 3-mm round crystal, three 15°s, one 6-mm round pearl, and one 15°. Run the needle back through the 6-mm pearl and all the other beads on the string. Put the needle through the adjacent Delica.

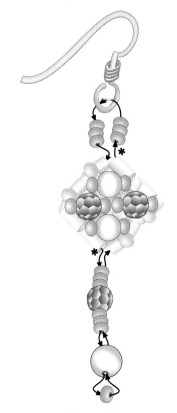

figure 17

18 Weave the needle through the RALS units to the point in between the bugle and Delica on the opposite corner of the beads just strung. With the needle coming out of the bugle as illustrated in the top portion of figure 17, pick up three 15°s, one ear wire, and three 15°s. Sew through the adjacent Delica. Weave in the thread, tie half-hitch knots, and cut it. Thread the tail, weave it in, tie half-hitch knots, and cut it.

Repeat all steps to make a second earring.

BRaCeLeTS

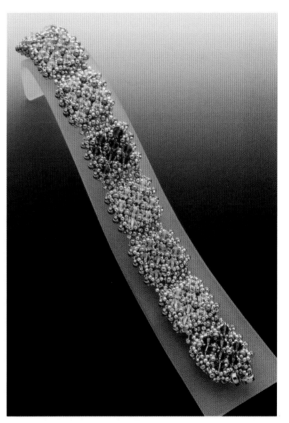

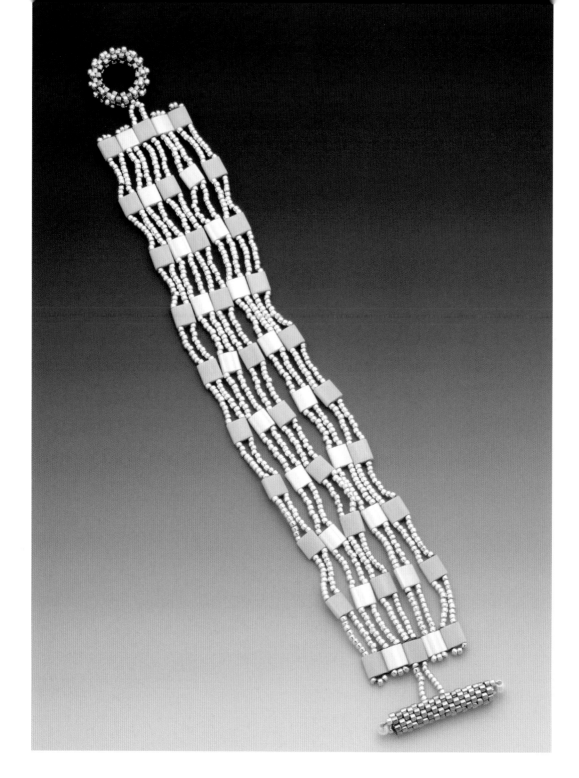

FAUX LIQUID SILVER BRACELET

Lately, I've seen many necklaces and bracelets made of silk cloth that look like strands of squares flowing together. Since trends are my thing, I decided to do a beaded version of this. As I was experimenting, I got something very different—the look of liquid silver. One of the most interesting parts of designing is encountering unexpected outcomes. It was rewarding to stumble upon something else when I had a different idea in mind.

SUPPLIES

Silver size 15° seed beads, 5 g

Tila beads:

    20–26 antique white (color A)

    30–36 matte opaque sky blue AB (color B)

FireLine 6 lb. test

Beading needles, size 12

CLASP SUPPLIES

Silver size 15° seed beads, 1 g

Silver size 11° Delicas, 1g

2 pearls, 3 mm

DIMENSIONS

7¼ inches (18.4 cm)

STITCH

Right angle weave variation

LEVEL

All Levels

Strands

1 Thread the needle with one and a half arm-lengths of thread. Leaving a 6-inch (15.2 cm) tail, pick up one color A and sew through both holes twice, leaving the tail on the top (figure 1).

figure 1

2 String on ten 15°s, pick up one color A, and put the needle through one hole, then the next (figure 2).

figure 2

3 Still referring to figure 2, string on ten 15°s. Put the needle back through both holes of the previous color A, the first ten 15°s strung, and the first hole of the second color A.

4 Repeat steps 2 and 3 until the strand is approximately ½ inch (12 mm) shorter than your wrist. Weave in the tail, tie half-hitch knots, and end it. Leave the working threads hanging on at least two completed strands.

5 Repeat steps 1 to 4, making three strands with color B and two strands with color A beads.

6 Line up the strands in the following order:
- Color B Tila bead
- Color A Tila bead
- Color B Tila bead
- Color A Tila bead
- Color B Tila bead

7 Using one of the remaining working threads on each side, sew the end Tila beads together side by side. Reinforce them several times to make sure they're secure (figure 3). Weave in the thread, tie half-hitch knots, and end it.

figure 3

8 Position the needle at the top of one of the end Tila beads. Pick up three 15°s and sew through the adjacent hole of the same Tila beads. Sew up through the hole of the next Tila bead. Pick up three 15°s and sew through the adjacent hole of the same Tila bead (figure 4).

figure 4

9 Repeat step 8 on the opposite side. Weave in the thread, tie half-hitch knots, and end it.

Clasp

10 Follow the directions on page 19 to make the Standard Clasp. For this project I stitched in all of the ditches in the circle portion of the clasp with 15°s.

11 Pick up the ring of the clasp and weave the needle through two 15°s in the center row. Pick up five 15°s. Put the needle through the three center 15°s at the top of B. Pick up five more 15°s. Put the needle back through the two 15°s in the circle. Reinforce it and put the needle through the top middle B as part of the reinforcement. Weave in the tail, tie half-hitch knots, and end it.

12 Pick up the toggle clasp. Weave the needle through the two center Delicas in the bar. Pick up eight 15°s. On the opposite side put the needle through the three 15°s atop of the center B. Pick up eight 15°s. Weave back through the two center Delicas in the bar clasp. Reinforce it. Then weave the needle through the top middle B as part of the reinforcement. Weave in the tail, tie half-hitch knots, and end it.

SUPPLIES

Silver size 11° Delicas, 7–10 g (depending upon wrist size)

Silver size 15° seed beads, 1.5 g

90–100 crystal AB round crystals, 2 mm

FireLine 6 lb. test

Beading needles, size 12

CLASP SUPPLIES

Silver size 15° seed beads, 1 g

Silver size 11° Delicas, 1 g

7 round crystals, 2 mm

2 white pearls, 3 mm

DIMENSIONS

7½ inches (7.5 cm)

STITCHES

Tubular herringbone stitch

Even-count tubular peyote stitch

Ladder stitch

LEVEL

All levels

KEEP YOUR COUNT STRAIGHT

Even-count tubular peyote stitch can be tricky. This tip will help you use the right quantity of beads in each row if you're new to the stitch. As you start each row, count out the number of beads you need and work with those. When you use the last bead that has been set aside, it's time to step up for the next row.

Bejeweled Barrel Bracelet

While some of the pieces I design come from ideas I see in metal, this one was truly my own. I loved the thought of crystal-encrusted barrels hugging a smooth tubular band. I also enjoy creating beaded beads and using the components in ways other than stringing. With this in mind, I tried to capture a rich look that is both simple and elegant.

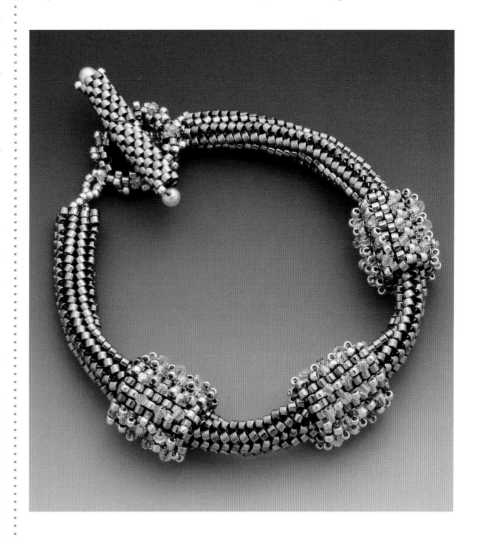

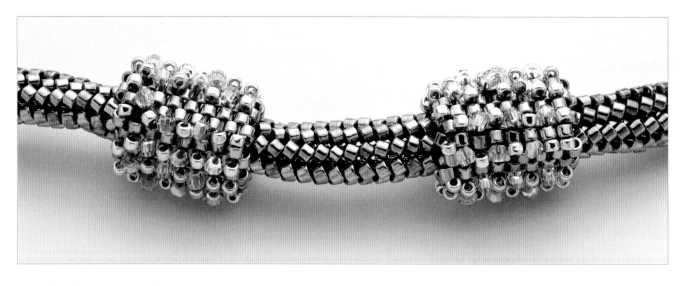

Herringbone Band

1 Thread the needle with one wing-span of thread and leave a 12-inch (30.5 cm) tail. Pick up two Delicas and ladder stitch them together. Continue to ladder stitch until there are eight Delicas in total in the ladder. Ladder stitch the first Delica to the last to make a ring.

2 Herringbone stitch a band approximately ½ inch (1.3 cm) shorter than the desired wrist length, adding thread as necessary. Remember to step up at the end of each row. When the band is the final size, weave the needle through the last two rows of herringbone several times to reinforce it. Leave the thread in place for now.

MIX IT UP

Not a big fan of crystals? Try substituting 11°s for the 2-mm round crystals that encrust the barrels. If you want contrast, use a different color 11° to achieve that. Or change the look in another way. Keep the design exactly the same with the crystals but bead a different color of 15° in the ditches to achieve a bit of contrast.

Make the Barrel Beads

3 Thread the needle with one wing-span of thread and leave a 6-inch (15.2 cm) tail. Pick up 20 Delicas and run the needle through the first three strung to make a ring.

4 Stitch even-count tubular peyote for 16 rows. (Keep in mind that the first two rows make three rows, and remember to step up at the end of each row.) Weave in the tail, tie half-hitch knots, and end it.

5 Move the needle down one Delica bead on the diagonal. Stitch in the ditch with 15°s all the way around, shown flat in figure 1 for clarity (figure 1).

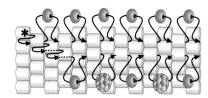

figure 1

6 Still referring to figure 1, move the needle down two Delica beads on the diagonal. Tie a half-hitch knot. Stitch in the ditch with one 15°, one 2-mm round crystal, one 15°, and one 2-mm round crystal, etc. Repeat the pattern all the way around.

7 Move the needle down two Delica beads on the diagonal. Stitch in the ditch with one 15°, one 2-mm round crystal, one 15°, and one 2-mm round crystal, etc. Repeat the pattern all the way around.

8 Repeat step 7 until you reach the last row (figure 2). For the last row, move the needle down one Delica bead on the diagonal in the base. Stitch in each ditch with one 15°.

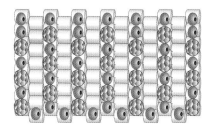

figure 2

9 Still referring to figure 2 as you make the last row, repeat step 5. Secure the piece by tying a half-hitch knot. Leave the thread in place for now. Make two more barrels, for a total of three.

Secure the Barrel Beads to the Band

10 Slide the three barrel beads onto the herringbone band of the bracelet. Center them and place them equal distances apart so that the three barrel beads will be visible on the front side of your wrist when you wear the bracelet.

11 Thread the needle onto the existing thread in the middle barrel bead. Weave the needle through the Delicas in the barrel bead to the middle. Tack down the barrel bead by putting the needle through the top of the barrel, the herringbone band, and the bottom of the barrel. Reinforce two or three times. Weave in the thread, tie half-hitch knots, and end it (figure 3).

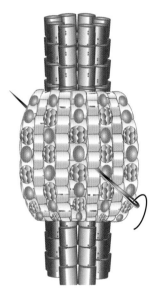

figure 3

12 Repeat step 11 to tack down the remaining barrel beads.

Make the Clasp

13 Follow the directions for the Standard Clasp (page 19), but substitute 15°s for the 11°s listed in the instructions.

Attach the Clasp

14 First attach the toggle, as follows. Thread the needle onto the remaining thread on one side of the herringbone band. Squeeze the herringbone flat, and move the needle so that it's coming out of the top of an end Delica (there should be four Delicas on the top and four on the bottom).

15 Pick up ten 15°s and put the needle through one Delica in the middle of the toggle. Pick up ten 15°s and put the needle through the opposite end of the same side of the herringbone band. Weave the needle through the herring-bone to the starting point, and put the needle back through the first set of ten 15°s, the toggle, and the second set of ten 15°s to reinforce it. Weave the thread into the herringbone band, tie half hitch knots, and end it.

16 Next you'll attach the ring part of the clasp. Repeat step 14 on the other end of the herringbone band. Pick up six 15°s and put the needle through two 15°s in the middle of the circle portion of the clasp. Pick up six 15°s and put the needle through the opposite side of the herringbone. Weave the needle through the herringbone to the starting point, and put the needle back through the first set of six 15°s, the circle, and the second set of six 15°s to reinforce it. Weave the thread into the herringbone band, tie half hitch knots, and end it.

Variation

animal instinct bracelet

One day I stopped in my local bead store and they were having a trunk show of fair trade beads. I was immediately drawn to the beads in a fun giraffe print! Then I learned that Kazuri, the company that produces them, employs more than 320 impoverished women in Africa, providing fair wages, health care, and childcare. This was a wonderful opportunity to create an elegant piece of jewelry while helping a worthwhile cause! I knew I had to use them in this book.

SUPPLIES

8 silver size 6° metal seed beads

Silver size 11° seed beads, 2 g

Silver size 11° Delicas, 8 g

4 flat bean-shaped clay beads (shales) in a giraffe print, 11 x 16 mm

120 crystal AB round crystals, 2 mm

2 white crystal pearls, 3 mm

FireLine 6 lb. test

Beading needles, size 12

Tape measure

CLASP SUPPLIES

Silver size 11° seed beads 1 g

Silver size 11° Delicas, 1 g

7 crystal AB round crystals, 2 mm

2 white pearls, 3 mm

DIMENSIONS

8 inches (20.3 cm)

STITCHES

Even-count tubular peyote stitch

Right angle weave (RAW)

LEVEL

Intermediate

WHY USE THE 6° SEED BEADS?

The Kazuri beads I used are called shales, made of clay from the Mt. Kenya area, and could crack if not properly mounted. To provide a little extra protection at the connection points, I strung a size 6° seed bead on either side of the hole. It's always a smart idea to protect your focal beads with something that isn't visually distracting.

Create the Circle Component

1 Thread the needle with one arm-length of thread. Pick up 32 Delicas and pass the needle through the first three to make a ring, making sure to leave a 6-inch (15.2 cm) tail.

2 Stitch even-count tubular peyote with Delicas for a total of five rows (the first two rows make three rows). Remember to step up at the end of each row. Thread the tail. Weave it in, tie half-hitch knots, and end it.

3 Refer to figure 1. Move the needle down one Delica on the diagonal through the base. Tie a half-hitch knot. Pick up one 2-mm round crystal and stitch in the ditch. Stitch each remaining ditch in the row with one 2-mm round crystal. Once the row is completed, move the needle down one Delica in the base on the diagonal.

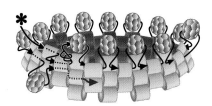

figure 1

4 Pick up one 11° seed bead and stitch in the ditch. Stitch in each remaining ditch in the row with one 11° seed bead (figure 2). Once the row is completed, move the needle down one Delica in the base on the diagonal.

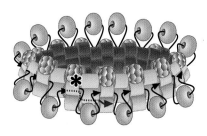

figure 2

5 Tie a half-hitch knot. Pick up one 2-mm round crystal and stitch in the ditch. Stitch each remaining ditch in the row with one 2-mm round crystal. Weave the needle so that it exits from an 11° seed bead in the center of the circle. Leave it in place for now (figure 3).

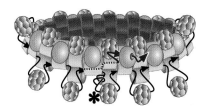

figure 3

6 Make four more identical circle components, for a total of five.

Assemble

7 Pick up one circle component. The needle should be positioned through an 11° in the center of the circle. Pick up one 6°, one giraffe shale, and one 6°.

8 Pick up a second circle component by weaving the needle through a center 11° in the second circle. Weave back through the 6°, the shale, the 6°, and the 11° on the first circle (figure 4).

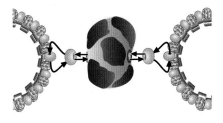

figure 4

9 Continue to weave the needle back and forth several times to tightly reinforce the clay bead between the two circle components. Weave it in, tie half-hitch knots, and end it.

10 Following steps 7–9, attach all five circles and all four shales to complete the body of the bracelet.

Variation

Create the Clasp

11 Follow the directions for the Standard Clasp on page 19, with the following changes. When making the ring component, stitch all three rows of ditches with 11°s. When adding the end pearls on the toggle component, pick up one 11°, one 3-mm pearl, and one 11° to complete. Leave the excess working thread hanging from each component once completed.

Attach the Clasp

12 Refer to figure 5. Thread the needle through 11°s in the center of the circle clasp. Pick up six 11°s and RAW, using two 11°s in the center of the circle clasp. Pick up six 11°s and do a second RAW stitch.

13 For the third RAW stitch, pick up two 11°s and sew through the two center 11°s on one of the end circle components. Pick up two more 11°s and complete the RAW stitch (figure 5).

figure 5

14 Reinforce by moving the needle through all three RAW stitches. Weave in the thread, tie half-hitch knots, and end it.

15 Refer to figure 6. Pick up the toggle and place it on the opposite end of the bracelet. Using the toggle thread, put the needle through two Delicas in the center of the toggle (figure 6).

figure 6

16 Pick up six 11°s and RAW. Pick up six 11°s and do a second RAW stitch. Follow steps 13 to 14 to complete the attachment.

FLORAL FANTASY BRACELET

Several years ago, I came across some beautiful hand-painted acrylic flowers. I started to collect them, but I couldn't figure out what to do with them. Some time later, I purchased a mix of Czech beads. My initial thought was to mix the flowers solely with something that sparkled. When I put the mix of the Czech beads and flowers together, the idea of a floral bracelet sprang to mind. To me this was an unlikely mix of more blended colors. I made note of this idea and put it aside for a while. The beads then started calling me. I knew I had to make this very bracelet with some variations from the idea in my head.

SUPPLIES

Picasso mix size 6° Czech seed beads, half a hank

Gold size 11° Delicas, 7 g

Gold size 11° seed beads, 5 g

Gold size 15° seed beads, 3 g

7 to 12 crystal AB round crystals, 4 mm

40 to 60 crystal AB round crystals, 2 mm

16 hand-painted acrylic flower and leaf beads, in various shapes, sizes, and colors

1 stopper bead

FireLine 6 lb. test

Beading needles, size 12

CLASP SUPPLIES

Gold size 15° seed beads, 1 g

Gold size 11° Delicas, 1g

7 crystal AB round crystal round, 2 mm

2 size 6° Picasso mix Czech seed beads

DIMENSIONS

7 1/4 inches (18.4 cm)

STITCHES

Flat peyote stitch

Even-count tubular peyote stitch

Right angle weave (RAW)

LEVEL

Intermediate

SIZING YOUR BRACELET

Every person has a different wrist size, so it's difficult to provide exact sizing instructions. Here are some things you can do to change the size.

To make the bracelet shorter, try making four decorative rings on each outer chain instead of five, and instead of ending the piece with one right angle weave unit, do three units. In other words, cut out the last circle in the chain and its attachment. Make the side bands shorter by stitching fewer rows of even-count peyote stitch.

To make the bracelet longer, add more rings to the outer chains. The side bands can also be made longer by stitching additional rows of even-count tubular peyote. Whether you stitch fewer or more rows of peyote stitch, remember to end on an even row.

Side Band

1 Thread the needle with one and a half arm-lengths of thread. Leaving a 6-inch (15.2 cm) tail with a stopper bead on the end, pick up 24 Delicas. Stitch flat peyote for 12 rows. Weave in both the tail and working thread, tie half-hitch knots, and end them. You've made one of the side bands. Make a second sideband by repeating this step.

Outer Chain 1

Rings

Cull through the 6° beads to find the smallest, most round ones. Keep those to use. Then make a total of six to fourteen rings depending on the length of your wrist, as follows. For the two rings to use on the ends, leave a 10-inch (25.4 cm) tail. For the other ones, leave a 6-inch (15.2 cm) tail. (Remember, you can add or subtract right angle weave units in between the rings to size the bracelet.)

2 Pick up 24 Delicas and put the needle through the first three to make a circle. Stitch even-count tubular peyote for five rows (remember the first two rows make three rows). Step up at the end of each row.

3 Move the needle down one Delica bead in the base on the diagonal. Stitch in each ditch with one 15° all the way around (figure 1).

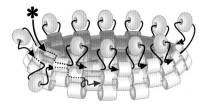

figure 1

4 Again move the needle down one Delica bead in the base on the diagonal. Repeat step 3 (figure 1).

MIX IT UP

The acrylic flowers come in a variety of colors so you can mix and match them to suit the accent beads of choice. Small gemstone beads would also look fabulous with the flowers. If you want more sparkle, substitute 4-mm round crystals for the Czech 6° beads, or make the piece with half crystals and half Czech 6° beads.

5 Move the needle down one Delica bead in the base on the diagonal and tie a half-hitch knot. Stitch in each ditch, alternating between one 15° and one 2-mm crystal (figure 2). For the two rings to use on the ends, leave the tail in place. For the others, weave in the tail, tie half-hitch knots, and end it.

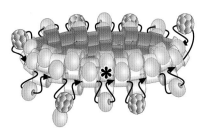

figure 2

Assembly

6 Follow figure 3. Pick up the working thread on one of the rings to use on the ends. Move the needle through the base and through two 15°s in the middle row of stitched ditches. Pick up six 11°s and make a right angle weave unit (using the two 15°s in the base as the first two beads in the unit). Pick up six 11°s and make a second right angle weave unit.

Continuing to follow figure 3, pick up two 11°s. Put the needle through two 15°s in the center of the ditches of the ring you just picked up. Pick up two 11°s. Do a right angle weave unit and reinforce it.

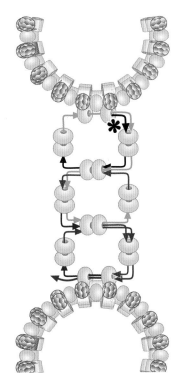

figure 3

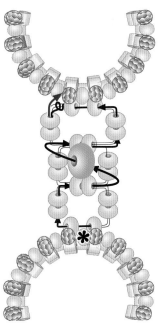

figure 4

7 Pick up one 6°. Put the needle through the top of the center right angle weave unit in the opposite direction. (The 6° should be placed in the center of the middle right angle weave unit, as shown in figure 4).

8 Still referring to figure 4, sew through the final right angle weave unit to reinforce it. Weave in the thread, tie half-hitch knots, and end it.

9 Thread the tail of the first ring. Pick up two 11°s. Put the needle through the two end Delicas on the side band. Pick up two 11°s. Put the needle through the two center 15°s in the middle of the ring. Reinforce the stitch several times. Weave in the thread, tie half-hitch knots, and end it (figure 5).

figure 5

10 Continue adding the rings to the chain following steps 6 through 8. When adding the final one, follow step 9, and attach it to the second side band. The piece should be approximately 1¾ inch (4.4 cm) shorter than your wrist.

Note: Make sure the rings line up straight across when attaching them together.

Outer Chain 2

11 Repeat steps 1 to 10 to make another—identical—outer chain, attaching it to the end two Delicas on the opposite end of the side band.

Inner Chain

12 Thread the needle with one wingspan of thread. Leaving a 10-inch (25.4 cm) tail, pick up eight 11°s and put the needle through all eight, and then through six more 11°s to position it for right angle weave. Pick up six 11°s and complete a second right angle weave unit. Continue adding right angle weave units until this strip is exactly the same length as the outer chains.

13 Thread the tail. Pick up two 11°s. Put the needle through the two center Delicas of one of the side bands; there should be three "up" Delicas between the innermost right angle weave unit on either end. Pick up two more 11°s and put the needle through the bottom two 11°s in the last right angle weave unit. Reinforce it several times. Weave in the thread. Tie half-hitch knots and end it.

14 Attach the other end of the inner chain to the second side bar in the same position as the first using the working thread. Do not end the thread (figure 6).

15 Embellish the inner chain by adding 4-mm crystals and 6° Czech beads as shown in figure 6.

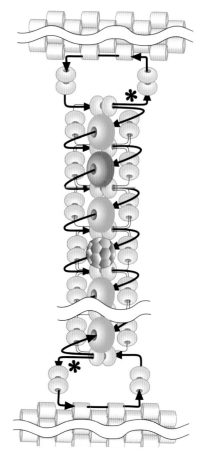

figure 6

Attach the Clasp

16 Follow the directions on page 19 for the Standard Clasp, but instead of adding pearls to the ends of the toggle, use 6° beads.

17 Attach the toggle to one end of the bracelet by picking up six 11°s. Right angle weave for four units. For the fifth unit, incorporate the two middle "up" Delicas of one of the side bands. Pass through the stitching several times to reinforce it, then weave in the thread, tie half-hitch knots, and end it.

18 Attach the ring to the opposite side bar by creating three right angle weave units with 11°s (the third unit will attach the ring and bar together). Pass through the stitching several times to reinforce it, then weave in the thread, tie half-hitch knots, and end it.

Attach the Flowers and Leaves

19 Thread the needle with one arm-length of thread and leave a 12-inch (30.5 cm) tail. Pick up four 15°s and sew through all four to make a ring. Move the needle through three 15°s so it's on the opposite side from the tail. Pick up three 15°s. Do a right angle weave stitch. Continue doing right angle weave stitches until you have eight right angle weave units. Put this strip of right angle weave around the bottom of any ring in either outer chain. Connect squares one and eight together by making a ninth right angle weave unit to form a connector (figure 7).

20 Thread the tail, pick up one 11°, one flower, one 11°, and a pleasing quantity of 15°s to make a calyx. Pick up one 6° and one 15°. Put the needle through the 6°, the 15°s, the 11°, the flower, and the 11°. Weave the thread through the right angle weave circle created, tie half-hitch knots, and end it (figure 8).

figure 8

The flower beads pictured here are painted by Heather French.

21 Make a right angle weave connector to fit each ring in the chain, as in step 19, and always attach it to the bottom portion of the ring. Add leaves and smaller flowers, as in step 20, using an eye-pleasing mix of 11°s, 15°s, and 6°s, always weaving back through the beads added and weaving in, tying off, and ending the thread in the right angle weave connector.

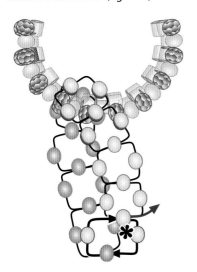

figure 7

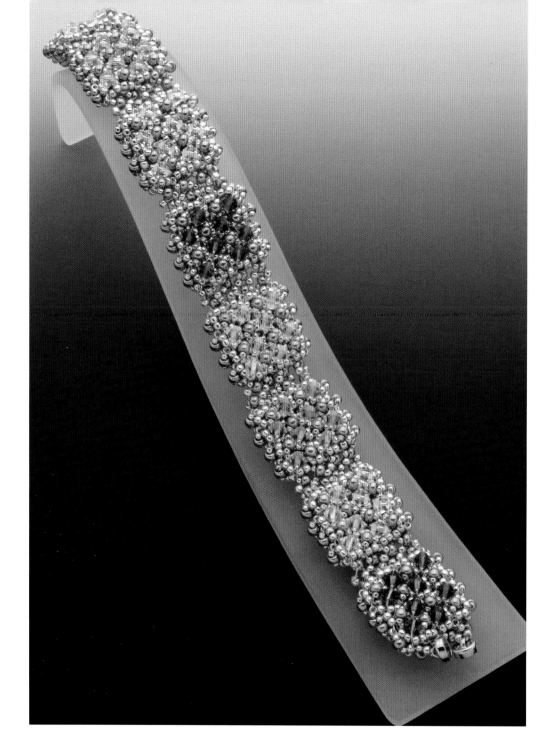

PILLOW TALK BRACELET

I am enamored with components and the variety of pieces that can be brought to life by using different stitches. One day I thought, "Instead of using a certain variation of RAW to embellish pieces as I normally do, why not make a component with the stitch?" So, after several tries, I came up with a square that reminded me of a pillow, and I decorated it with crystals. After stitching a few more similar pillows, I liked how the pieces fit together. Then I attached them to create this bracelet.

SUPPLIES

Gold size 8° seed beads, 8 g

Gold size 11° seed beads, 15 g

Gold size 15° seed beads, 3.2 g

32 crystal bicones, 4 mm (color A)

16 light turquoise bicones, 4 mm (color B)

16 tanzanite bicones, 4 mm (color C)

2 magnetic round clasps, 6 mm

FireLine 6 lb. test

Beading needles, size 12

DIMENSIONS

8 inches (20.3 cm)

STITCHES

Right angle weave (RAW)

LEVEL

Intermediate

Make the Pillows

1 Thread the needle with one wingspan of thread, leaving a 6-inch tail (15.2 cm).

2 Pick up eight 11° seed beads and run the needle back through all of them to create a ring. Move the needle through six of these beads to position it for RAW.

3 Create four RAW units with 11°s. After the fourth unit, step up and stitch eight more rows for a total of nine (figure 1).

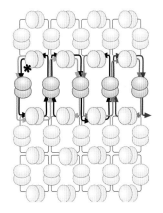

figure 1

Note: Refer to figure 1 for steps 4 through 7.

4 Zip row 1 to row 9. To do so, pick up two 11° seed beads and pass the needle through the end two 11°s of row one. Pick up two 11°s and run the needle through the end two 11°s in row nine again. Weave to the end two 11°s of the next RAW unit in row 9.

Pick up two 11°s and complete a new RAW unit. Weave around to position the needle for the third unit. Pick up two 11°s and create the third RAW unit. For the final unit, all four sides of RAW will be in place. Reinforce the stitch by weaving the thread through it.

5 Zip the remaining two sides of RAW to create an enclosed square (pillow), using two 11°s in three stitches to complete each side.

6 Once zipped, weave to the back of the completed pillow. Add thread as necessary.

Repeat to make an additional five to seven pillows, depending on the length of your bracelet.

Decorate the Pillow

Note: Before going further, choose one side of the bracelet to be the front, which will show your decorative enhancements. Refer to the opposite side as the back.

7 Selecting one of the pillows, position the needle so that it is coming out of one row on one end of the back.

8 Pick up one 15° seed bead, one 8° seed bead, and one 15°. Sew through the opposite side of the unit in the opposite way so that the 8° lies in the middle (figure 2).

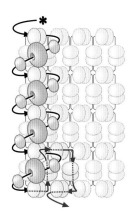

figure 2

9 Repeat Step 8 until all the RAW units are filled in on the back (figure 3).

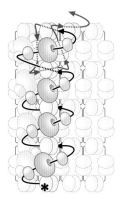

figure 3

10 Move the needle to the side of the pillow. Repeat Step 8 until all the RAW units on all four sides are filled with one 15°, one 8°, and one 15° (figure 4).

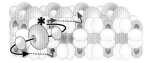

figure 4

11 Move the needle to the front of the pillow. With the needle coming out of a pair of 11°s on one of the end units, repeat step 9. For the next stitch, pick up one of the color A, B, or C bicones and stitch into the opposite side of the unit in the opposite way so the bicone lies in the middle of a RAW unit (figure 5).

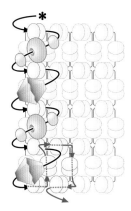

figure 5

Note: Each pillow is made with one color bicone. It does not matter which color you begin with. Follow the guide

in Step 13 for the total number of pillows in each color.

12 Repeat step 11 to finish the row. Then weave your thread around to the adjacent unit in the next row (figure 6).

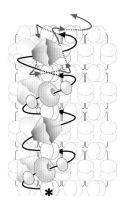

figure 6

13 Repeat steps 11 and 12 until all of the units are filled in with the alternating pattern (figure 6).

Make the following pillows, leaving the remaining thread in place once completed:

- Color A: four pillows
- Color B: two pillows
- Color C: two pillows

Note: For small wrists, create fewer pillows. For large wrists, create more pillows.

Attaching the Pillows

14 Line up the pillows in the following order based on bicone colors:

- color A, color B, color A, color C, color A, color B, color A, color C

Note: Make sure the pillows face in the same direction and that the diagonal lines of all look like a unified pattern.

Refer to figure 7 for steps 15–19.

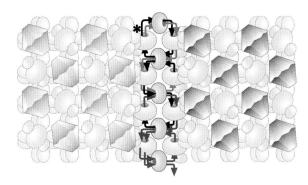

figure 7

15 Pick up one color A and one color B pillow. Arrange them side-by-side with 8° seed beads facing each other. (Ignore the two 15°s on each side of the 8°s). Weave an existing thread to where the side rows meet.

16 Weave the needle through the first 8° in the A pillow. Pick up one 11°. Sew through one 8° in the B pillow. Pick up one 11° and sew through the first 8° in the A pillow. Reinforce it once.

17 Weave the needle through the RAW in the first A pillow and position it through the second side 8°. Repeat Step 16.

18 Repeat step 16 until all four 8°s on the side are sewn together with a separate RAW stitch.

19 Attach all eight pillows in a row following steps 16 and 17, but alternating the colors of the pillows as indicated in step 14.

Attach the Clasps

20 The two end pillows each contain four 8° seed beads on their unattached sides. If thread exists, weave it through the RAW so that it is between the top two 8°s. If there is no existing thread, add approximately 18 inches (45.7 cm).

21 Pick up one 11°, one half of a magnetic clasp, and one 11°. Sew through the next 8° on the side of the pillow. Weave through the RAW and reinforce it several times. Continue by weaving through the RAW between the bottom two 8°s. Pick up the other half of the magnetic clasp and repeat the step. Weave in the thread, tie half-hitch knots, and cut it off (figure 8).

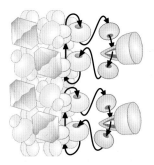

figure 8

22 Repeat Steps 20 and 21 on the opposite end of the bracelet.

Tennis Bracelet Trio

One day, I was playing around with cubic RAW, trying unsuccessfully to get it to stay stiff. I decided that a different approach was necessary, and a thought soon sprang to mind. Why not combine the classic stitch with ladder stitch, using size 1 bugle beads to obtain the desired texture? Ever since, I can't get enough of what I call right angle ladder stitch (RALS). It's very exciting to discover a stitch combination! To teach the basic stitch, I wanted a simple yet classic project, hence this trio of bracelets. No jewelry collection is complete without a tennis bracelet. It's essential to a wardrobe.

SUPPLIES

Gold Bracelet

Size 11° seed beads:

one shade of gold, 1.5 g (color A)

a second shade of gold, 1.5 g (color B)

Gold size 11° Delicas, 2 g

Light beige Apollos size 1 bugle beads, 1 g

5 crystal AB round crystals, 4 mm

1 white round crystal pearl, 8 mm

FireLine 6 lb. test

Beading needle, size 12

Silver Bracelet

Size 11° seed beads:

silver, 1.5 g (color A)

nickel, 1.5 g (color B)

Silver size 11° Delicas, 2 g

Nickel size 1 bugle beads, 1 g

5 crystal AB round crystals, 4 mm

1 white round crystal pearl, 8 mm

FireLine 6 lb. test

Beading needles, size 12

Copper Bracelet

Size 11° seed beads:

One shade of copper, 1.5 g (color A)

Another shade of copper, 1.5 g (color B)

Copper size 11° Delicas, 2 g

Turquoise Apollos size 1 bugle beads, 1 g

5 crystal AB round crystals, 4 mm

1 white round crystal pearl, 8 mm

FireLine 6 lb. test

Beading needles, size 12

DIMENSIONS

6⅞ inches (17.4 cm)

STITCHES

Right angle ladder stitch (RALS)

Even-count peyote

LEVEL

Intermediate

Note: The instructions are the same no matter which color bracelet you're making.

FOLLOW THE PATH

As you start the RALS, you'll realize that there are several ways to run the thread path. While learning the stitch, I strongly advise that you follow the thread path shown in the illustrations. If you take your own path, it can change they way the units fit together and flow.

RALS Base

1 Thread the needle onto one wingspan of thread and leave a 10-inch (25.4 cm) tail.

Front of the First Square

2 Pick up two bugle beads and ladder stitch them together one time, so they lie side by side. Orient your beadwork as shown in figure 1.

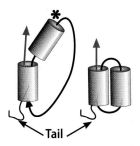

figure 1

3 As shown in figure 2, pick up one Delica, one A, and one Delica (this will be called Group 1). Pick up two more bugles. Ladder stitch them together one at a time, so they lie side by side.

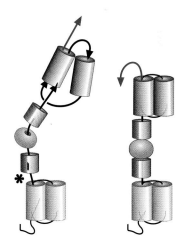

figure 2

4 With the needle coming out of the new bugle, pick up another Group 1. Stitch through the starting bugle on the side opposite of where the tail thread is coming out of to complete the front of the square. Ladder up through the adjacent bugle without adding any beads (figure 3).

figure 3

Back of the First Square

5 With the needle coming out of the back bugle, pick up one Delica, one B, and one Delica (this is Group 2). Stitch through the next back bugle on the side opposite of where the thread is coming out. Pick up one Group 2. Stitch through the first back bugle to complete the back of the square-shaped unit (figure 4).

figure 4

6 Weave the needle through the Group 2 beads and the next bugle. Ladder up without beads through the adjacent bugle to the front to be in position for the next unit (figure 5).

figure 5

Second Square

7 Flip the beadwork over; you'll now work on the front. With the needle coming out of the front bugle, pick up one Group 1 and two bugles. Ladder stitch the bugles together one at a time, to lie side by side (figure 6).

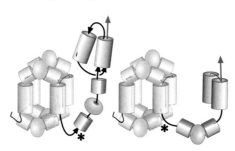

figure 6

8 Pick up Group 1 and sew through the front bugle of the first unit. Ladder up through the adjacent bugle without adding any beads to the back (figure 7).

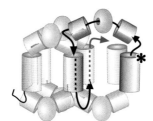

figure 7

9 Flip the beadwork over and pick up one Group 2 and sew through the next back bugle. Pick up a second Group 2 and sew through the back bugle of the first unit (figure 8).

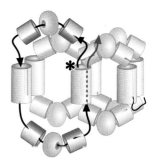

figure 8

10 Weave the needle through Group 2 and the next bugle. Ladder up through the adjacent bugle without adding any beads (figure 9).

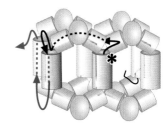

figure 9

MIX IT UP

There are many ways to change the look of these bracelets. Instead of adding on just a few crystals, try putting a 4-mm round crystal in every other RALS square for the bling effect. Change the colors of the crystals, or try a rainbow effect. If you don't want to use crystals at all, 4-mm gemstones or pearls will work perfectly in this arrangement. And if three-tone isn't your look, create three bracelets in a single color.

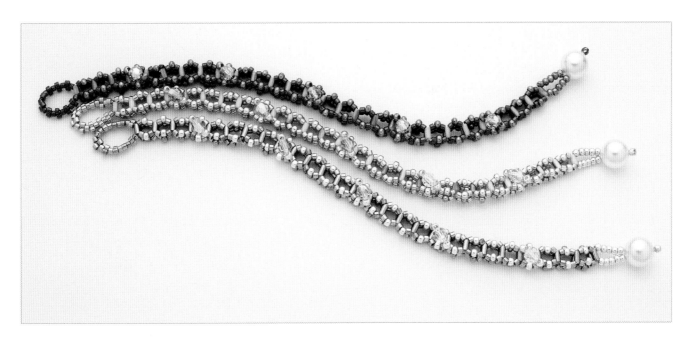

Third Square

11 Pick up Group 1 and two bugles. Ladder stitch the bugles together so they lie side by side (figure 10).

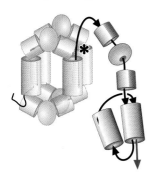

figure 10

12 Pick up Group 1 and stitch through the next bugle, then ladder down to the adjacent bugle without adding any beads (figure 11).

figure 11

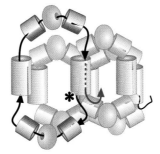

figure 12

13 Flip the beadwork over. Pick up one Group 2 and stitch through the next bugle. Pick up another Group 2 and stitch through the next bugle (figure 12).

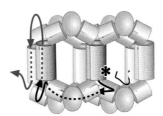

figure 13

14 Stitch through the first Group 2 and bugle. Then ladder to the adjacent bugle without adding any beads (figure 13).

15 Repeat steps 7 to 14, adding thread as necessary, until the bracelet is approximately ¼ inch (6 mm) shorter than the desired length.

Loop Closure

16 Weave the thread through the top bugle on the front side. String on 20 Delicas and put the needle through the opposite end of the same bugle. Using Delicas, stitch one row of even-count tubular peyote through these beads as shown in figure 14.

Note: Your thread placement will alternate in every other stitch as in right angle weave.

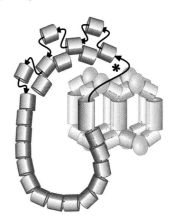

figure 14

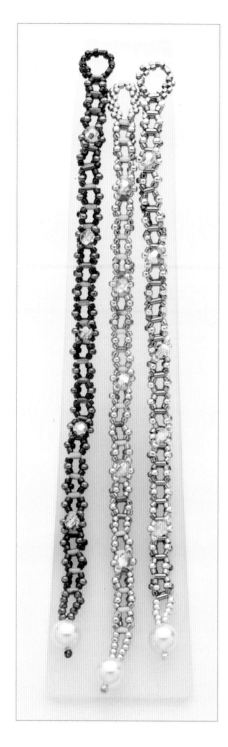

Embellish the Base

17 Count the number of right angle ladder stitches in the bracelet. Decide how to space out the 4-mm crystals. Weave the needle through the top of the RALS (through the Group 1s) and position it where the first crystal will be placed.

18 Pick up one A, one 4-mm crystal, and one A. Weave the needle into the next top bugle the opposite way (figure 15).

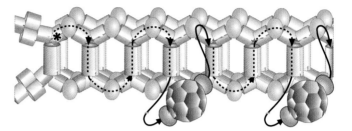

figure 15

19 Weave the needle through the top of the RALS (through the Group 1s) and position it where the next crystal will be placed. Pick up one A, one 4-mm crystal, and one A. Weave the needle into the next top bugle the opposite way. Repeat until you've attached all the crystals. Weave in the thread, tie half-hitch knots, and end it.

Pearl Clasp

20 Thread the tail and weave through the top end bugle on the front side. Pick up five As and the pearl. Pick up one A and put the needle back through the pearl. Pick up five As and put the needle through the opposite side of the top bugle (figure 16). Weave through these beads again to reinforce. Weave in the thread, tie half-hitch knots, and end it.

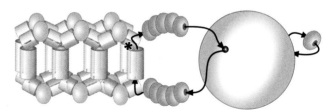

figure 16

OPPOSITES ATTRACT BRACELET

This reversible bracelet, gold on one side and silver on the other, is created with a special stitch I developed, which I call right angle ladder stitch. Bead it up and you'll feel like you made two projects in the time of just one—such a treat for seed beaders! Stun your friends with this beauty.

SUPPLIES

Gold size 11° seed beads, 3–4 g

Size 1 bugle beads

gold, 2.5–4 g* (color A)

nickel, 2.5–5 g* (color B)

Size 11° Delicas

gold, 2.5–3 g (color C)

silver, 2–3.5 g (color D)

200–300 clear AB round crystals, 2 mm

FireLine 6 lb. test

Beading needles, size 12

* Amount will depend on wrist size

CLASP SUPPLIES

Silver size 11° seed beads, 1 g

Silver size 11° Delicas, 1g

Gold size 11° Delicas, 1g

Silver size 15° seed beads, 1g

Gold size 15° seed beads, 1g

2 white pearls, 3 mm

14 crystal AB round crystals, 2 mm

DIMENSIONS

6½ inches (16.5 cm), excluding clasp

STITCHES

Right angle ladder stitch (RALS)

LEVEL

Advanced

STITCHING THE FRONT AND BACK

While stitching the bracelet, think of it as beading two-sided right angle weave squares. Because of the addition of the ladder stitch, you are actually working separately to complete the front and the back of the bracelet. Instead of doing right angle weave once for each stitch, you're actually doing it twice.

RALS Base Row

Front of the First Square Unit

1 Thread the needle onto one wingspan of thread. Leaving a 6-inch (15.2 cm) tail, pick up one A and one B and ladder stitch them together once so they lie side by side (figure 1).

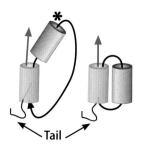

figure 1

2 Pick up one C, one 11°, and one C (this pattern will be called Group 1). Using the same thread, pick up one A and one B and ladder stitch them together so they align with the A and B on the opposite side (figure 2).

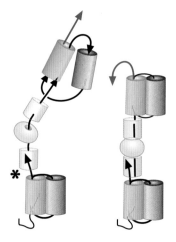

figure 2

3 With the needle coming out of A, pick up another Group 1. Stitch through the A on the opposite side to complete the top of the square unit (figure 3).

figure 3

4 Still referring to figure 3, ladder stitch down through the B without adding any beads.

Back of the First Square Unit

5 With the needle coming out of the B, pick up one D, one crystal, and one D (this pattern will be called Group 2). Stitch through the next B on the side opposite where the thread is coming out. Repeat to complete the back of the square-shaped unit (figure 4).

figure 4

6 With the needle coming out of the B (the starting point on the bottom), move it through the next Group 2 and the next B. Ladder stitch up through the B and down through the A to position it for the next unit (figure 5).

figure 5

Additional Square Units in the Base Row

7 Flip the beadwork over to the front, and pick up Group 1. Pick up A, then B, and ladder stitch them together so they lie side by side (figure 6).

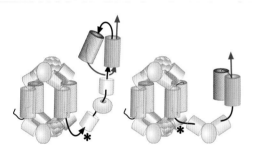

figure 6

8 Pick up Group 1 and sew through the A. Ladder stitch up to B without adding any beads (figure 7).

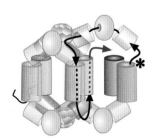

figure 7

9 Flip the beadwork over to the back. Pick up Group 2 and sew through the next B (figure 8).

figure 8

10 Still referring to figure 8, pick up a second Group 2 and sew through the last B.

11 Stitch through Group 2 and one B. Ladder stitch to A without adding any beads (figure 9).

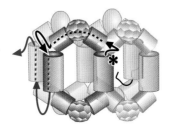

figure 9

12 Pick up one Group 1, one A, and one B. Ladder stitch the A and B together (figure 10).

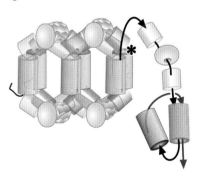

figure 10

13 Pick up one Group 1. Stitch through the next A, then ladder to B without adding any beads (figure 11).

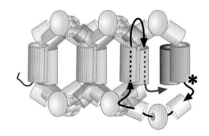

figure 11

14 Pick up one Group 2 and stitch through the next B. Pick up another Group 2 and stitch through the next B (figure 12).

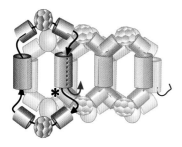

figure 12

15 Stitch through the Group 1 and the next B. Ladder to the A without adding any beads (figure 13).

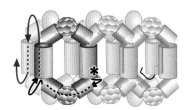

figure 13

16 Follow steps 7 to 15 to make a row approximately 1½ inches (3.8 cm) shorter than the desired length. For the very last unit, move the needle through Group 2 and ladder stitch up without adding any beads) to Group 1. This will position the needle for the next row. Weave in the tail, tie half-hitch knots, and end it.

Note: Your thread placement will alternate in every other stitch as in right angle weave.

Row 2

Square Unit 1

17 Weave the needle so it's exiting from the left side of Group 1 at the top. Ladder stitch together one A and one B (figure 14).

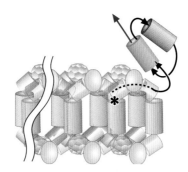

figure 14

18 Pick up Group 1 (figure 15).

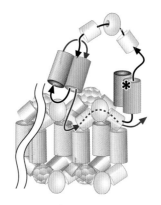

figure 15

19 Still referring to figure 15, ladder stitch together one A and one B. Put the needle through the existing Group 1 from the previous row to complete this side of the unit.

20 Flip the beadwork over. Put the needle through Group 2 on the previous row and through B. Pick up Group 2. Put the needle through B, the next Group 2 and the next B. Ladder stitch to A (figure 16).

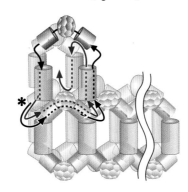

figure 16

Square Unit 2

21 Flip the beadwork over. Stitch through Group 1. Ladder stitch together one A and one B (figure 17).

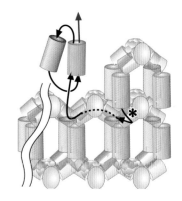

figure 17

22 Pick up one Group 1 and stitch through A. Put the needle through Group 1 and A (figure 18).

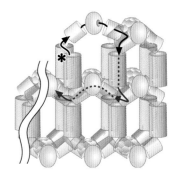

figure 18

23 Flip the beadwork over. Stitch through the Group 2 and B. Pick up one Group 2. Sew through B and then Group 2 in the previous row, B, and the newly added Group 2. Move the needle through B and ladder to A (figure 19).

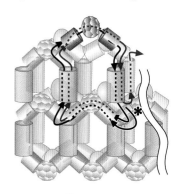

figure 19

Square Unit 3

24 Flip the beadwork over. Pick up one Group 1 and ladder stitch together one A and one B. Stitch through Group 1 and the next A (figure 20).

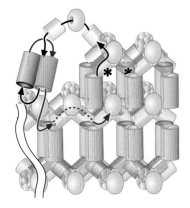

figure 20

25 Flip the beadwork over. Stitch through the adjacent Group 2 and B. Pick up Group 2 and stitch through the next B. Then stitch through the Group 2 and the next B then ladder stitch to B (figure 21).

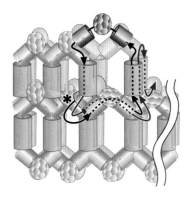

figure 21

26 Repeat steps 21 to 25 until the row is complete. Make a total of six rows of right angle ladder stitch.

Clasp

27 Follow the directions on page 19 to make a Standard Clasp, making the toggle gold and the ring silver to match the two sides of the piece.

Attach the Clasp

Toggle

28 Weave the remaining thread on the toggle through one middle Delica.

29 Pick up eight 11°s and put the needle through the end bugles in rows 3 and 4. This toggle can be anchored to either the top or bottom.

30 Pick up eight 11°s and sew back through the Delica on the toggle. Sew back through the attachment several times to reinforce. Weave in the thread, tie half-hitch knots, and end.

Ring

31 Weave the excess thread from the ring into two middle size 11°s. Pick up five 11°s and put the needle through the end bugles in rows 3 and 4, choosing the same position as step 26.

32 Pick up five 11°s and sew back through the 11°s on the ring. Sew back through the attachment several times to reinforce. Weave in the thread, tie half-hitch knots, and end it.

MIX IT UP

If you want to add more color to the piece, substitute the 2-mm round crystals and the more demure 11°s for bright color 11°s, one matching the silver tone and the other matching the gold tone. This will give the piece more flash.

SUPPLIES

Apricot gold size 11° seed beads, 12 g

Gold size 15° seed beads, 0.5 g

5 Bakelite rings, 1⅛ inch (2.8 cm) in diameter

36 pale pink crystal pearls, 3 mm

FireLine 6 lb. test

Beading needles, size 12

DIMENSIONS

32 inches (81.3 cm)

STITCHES

Right angle weave (RAW)

LEVEL

Beginner

CHAIN GANG

You can change the length of the necklace by making the seed bead chains and the neck strap longer or shorter. It's important to make sure all of the seed bead chains (separating the Bakelite rings) are exactly the same length, so keep count of the number of units you make. You can make several necklaces of different lengths and wear them all together for a dramatic look.

FULL CIRCLE NECKLACE

I like the idea of combining a little something from the past with contemporary flair. When I saw these vintage Bakelite rings on display, I instantly invented this necklace in my mind. In fact, this is the only design in this book that was successful as a very first take. I knew exactly how to put it together because it's easy to make. Not every beautiful piece has to be difficult.

Seed Bead Chain and Neck Strap

The neck strap is the element worn around the back of the neck, while the seed bead chains link the Bakelite rings in the front. Both are made in identical fashion, but the neck strap will be longer than the seed bead chain.

1 Thread the needle with one wingspan of thread. Leaving an 8-inch (20.3 cm) tail, pick up eight 11°s and run the needle through them all to make a ring (figure 1).

figure 1

2 Run the needle through six more 11°s so that it's on the opposite side from the tail.

Note: Visualize the beads as a square shape, with two 11° beads on each side of the square. This square is one RAW unit.

3 Pick up six 11°s. Run the needle through the top two 11°s of the previous unit, and then through four additional 11°s to weave it to the top of the current unit. Repeat until you've made 30 units total.

Note: Figure 2 shows the second and third RAW units being added. (figure 2).

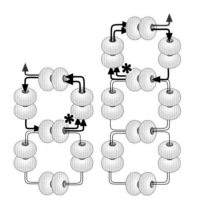

figure 2

Note: The needle position will alternate sides each time as the units are created.

4 You've finished one seed bead chain. Make three more identical ones, for a total of four. Then make one chain 64 units long; this will be the neck strap.

Attach the Chain to the Rings

5 Slip just the end of one of the short seed bead chains—the end with the working thread on it—around one of the Bakelite rings. Count out six units from the end (row 24). Pick up two 11°s and stitch through the top of that row (between units 6 and 7). Pick up two 11°s. Move the needle through the top side of the end unit to complete it (figure 3). Reinforce it once.

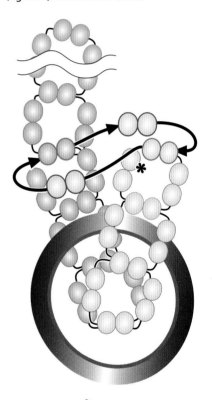

figure 3

78

6 Leaving the working thread in place, thread the tail and repeat step 4 using the tail thread and another Bakelite ring. Weave in the tail, tie half-hitch knots, and end it.

7 Go back to using the working thread. Position the needle so that it's coming out of the top of the first square that's not part of the loop around the Bakelite ring. Pick up one 15°, one pearl, and one 15°. Sew through the top of the next unit in the opposite direction. Then sew through the side and top of the next unit. Repeat until there are nine pearls attached in every other RAW stitch (figure 4). Weave in the thread, tie half-hitch knots, and end it.

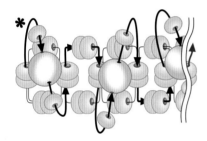

figure 4

8 Using the short seed bead chains, link the remaining Bakelite rings consecutively to the existing set and embellish with pearls as described above. Once completed, you should have a ring at each end of a long chain.

Note: Make sure the pearls face the same way on each strap.

Finish

9 Attach the neck strap to the rings at the end of the long chain as described in step 5. Make sure the neck strap isn't twisted.

10 Sew through all 64 RAW units without adding any beads to reinforce it. Weave in the thread, tie half-hitch knots, and end it.

BeaDettes necklace

The potential for beading bliss is limitless once your mind begins to roam around an idea like using these beadettes in a necklace (as I did here) or in other pieces. You can decorate them freeform by randomly adding beads in the ditches, or make a pattern—they look great either way. Enjoy the creative process of integrating these pieces into your work. You will find them to complement so many of the designs in this book.

SUPPLIES

(Makes three beaded beads)

Metallic plum size 11° seed beads, 2.5 g (color A)

Gold size 11° seed beads, 6–8 g (color B)

Gold size 11° Delicas, 3 g

Gold size 15° seed beads, 2.5 g

60 black round agates, 2 mm

35–40 crystal AB round crystals, 2 mm

FireLine 6 lb. test

Beading needles, size 12

CLASP SUPPLIES

Gold size 11° seed beads, 1 g

Gold size 11° Delicas, 1 g

4 gold size 15° seed beads

2 white pearls, 3 mm

DIMENSIONS

18³⁄₄ inches (47.6 cm)

STITCHES

Even-count tubular peyote stitch

Fringe stitch

Right angle weave (RAW)

LEVEL

All Levels

DARK BEADS

I feel that using a dark accent bead on either end of this piece lends character. I used 2-mm round agates, but any dark bead similar in size to an 11° seed bead will serve. This includes 2-mm round crystals, pearls, fire-polished, etc. Go though your treasure box and find some things that haven't been used recently to add the perfect touches.

Create the Base for a Beaded Bead

1 Thread the needle with one arm-length of thread and leave a six-inch (15.2 cm) tail. Pick up 20 Delicas and put the needle through the first three to make a circle.

2 Stitch in even-count tubular peyote stitch for 18 rows. (Remember the first two rows make three rows.) Step up at the end of each row.

Decorate the Base

Note: The drawings in figures 1 and 2 are shown flat for easy reference.

Refer to figure 1 for steps 3 through 5.

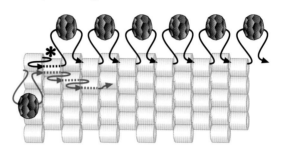

figure 1

3 With the needle coming out of a top Delica, move it down one Delica bead on the diagonal.

4 Stitch in each ditch in the row with one 2-mm round agate.

5 Move the needle down two Delicas on the diagonal.

6 Pick up two 15° seed beads, one A, and two more 15°s and stitch in each ditch in the row. To give the piece a little sparkle, substitute one 2-mm round crystal for an A once every four to six stitches (figure 2).

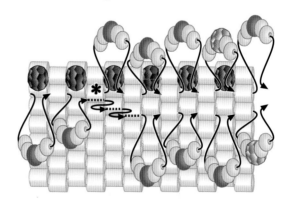

figure 2

7 Repeat steps 5 and 6 five more times for six rows in total.

8 Move the needle down one Delica bead on the diagonal. Repeat step 4.

9 Weave in the thread, tie half-hitch knots, and end it.

10 Make two more beaded beads for a total of three.

Make the Clasp

11 Follow the directions for the Standard Clasp on page 19.

Make the Chain

12 Thread the needle using one wingspan of thread, leaving a 10-inch (25.4 cm) tail. Pick up eight Bs and string the needle through all to create a unit. Continue stringing the needle through six Bs to position it for RAW.

figure 3

13 Pick up six Bs. String the needle through the top two Bs on the previous unit and the next four in the new unit. Continue creating RAW units until the chain reaches your desired length (I did 16½ inches, 42 cm).

Attach the Clasp

14 Thread the tail. Pick up two Bs and string the needle through two Delicas in the middle of the toggle component of the clasp. Pick up two Bs and string the needle through the top RAW unit. Reinforce it several times (figure 3).

15 Place the beaded beads on the chain first. Using the excess thread on the end of the chain, pick up two Bs. String the needle through two middle beads in the ring component of the clasp. Pick up two Bs and put the needle through the top RAW unit. Reinforce it several times.

16 Weave in the threads on both sides, tie half-hitch knots, and end it.

cameo de oro pendant

Cameos are fascinating silhouettes that no fine jewelry wardrobe should be without. They are special because each has a different personality. In fact, when I saw this one, it virtually screamed, "Pick me, choose me!"

I wanted the facing rather than the beadwork to be the focal point for this intriguing piece. Surrounding the cameo with glass pearls, crystals, and metal seed beads creates a rich-looking setting. One of the tough things when creating many jewelry pieces is deciding what part of the piece should stand out most. Cameos, however, make that decision for you. They practically talk to you and ask for a look worthy of their detail.

SUPPLIES

Gold size 11° seed beads, 1 g

Gold size 11° Delicas, 0.5 g

Gold size 15° seed beads, 0.5 g

20–30 crystal AB round crystals, 2 mm

40–50 white Czech pearls, 2 mm

1 cameo pendant

Stiff beading foundation, cut to size

Synthetic suede, cut to size

Craft adhesive

FireLine 6 lb. test

Beading needles, size 12

DIMENSIONS

1³⁄₄ inches (4.5 cm)

STITCHES

Bead embroidery

Even-count tubular peyote stitch

Right angle weave (RAW)

LEVEL

Intermediate

TIPS & TRICKS

The true wonder of bead embroidery is that it doesn't have "rules" like many other stitches. Cut your stiff beading foundation so it is ½ inch (1.3 cm) wider than the cameo. You may decide to add extra embellishments to a piece like this, such as seed beads, small gemstones, or extra crystals—do whatever pleases your own sense of style.

Embroider the Cameo

1 Cut a piece of beading foundation approximately ½ inch (1.3 cm) wider on all sides than the cameo and use adhesive to glue the cameo in the center. Let it dry for at least 20 minutes.

2 Thread a needle with one and a half arm-lengths of thread and tie a thick knot at the end.

3 Following the black thread path in figure 1, pass the needle from the back side of the glued cameo so it comes up through the front next to the cameo. Pick up two Delicas and pass the needle back down through the foundation. Following the red thread path in figure 1, continue by sewing up again through the foundation and through the two Delicas.

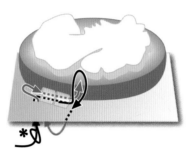

figure 1

4 Pick up two Delicas and pass the needle back down through the foundation (figure 2, black thread path). Continue by sewing up again to the front of the foundation and through the second Delica of the first stitch plus the two Delicas just added (figure 2, red thread path).

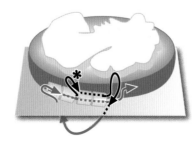

figure 2

5 Repeat step 4 until there is an even count of Delicas surrounding the cameo.

6 Stitch even-count tubular peyote for four to seven rows (depending on the depth of the cameo). Remember to step up at the end of each row (figure 3).

figure 3

7 When reaching the top of the cameo, stitch one final row of even-count tubular peyote with 15° seed beads (figure 4).

figure 4

8 Move the needle down one Delica bead on the diagonal in the base. Tie a half-hitch knot and stitch in each ditch of the row, alternating one 11° seed bead and one round crystal (figure 5). When completed, weave the thread through the foundation to the back, knot it, and cut it (figure 5).

figure 5

9 Thread the needle with one arm-length of thread and tie a thick knot at the end.

10 Following the black thread path in figure 6, sew through the foundation from back to front close to the base of the cameo bezel and pick up two pearls, positioning them flush to the Delicas on the bottom row of the bead embroidery. Then pass the needle down through the foundation.

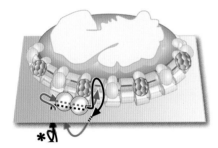

figure 6

11 Following the red path in figure 6, sew up through the foundation and again through the two pearls.

12 As shown by the black thread path in figure 7, pick up two more pearls and sew down through the foundation. Continue by sewing up again to the front of the foundation and through the second pearl of the first pearl stitch plus the two pearls just added.

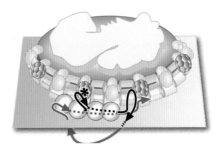

figure 7

13 Repeat step 12 until circling around to the first pearl, where you will thread the needle through the first and last pearl.

Note: You can continue to sew through several pearls to anchor them. Weave the thread through the foundation to the back, knot it, and cut it.

14 Cut a piece of synthetic suede approximately ¼ inch (6 mm) in diameter larger than the foundation and glue it to the back of the foundation. Let it dry for at least 20 minutes. Then cut the suede and foundation backing around the cameo, as close to the piece as possible, being careful not to cut any threads.

15 Thread the needle with one arm-length of thread and tie a knot at the end. Position the needle between the suede and the foundation and pass it through to the front of the foundation.

16 Pick up one 15° seed bead, one 11° seed bead, and another 15°. Sew down through the suede and foundation (figure 8 left, black thread path). Then sew through the last 15° added (figure 8 left, red thread path).

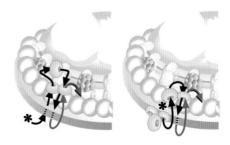

figure 8

17 Pick up one 11° seed bead and one 15° (figure 8 right, black thread path). Sew down through the suede and foundation, then back through the last 15° added (figure 8 right, red thread path).

18 Repeat step 17 until there are picots all the way around the cameo. For the last stitch, add one 11° in between the two existing 15°s in the first and last picot. Weave the remaining thread to the top of the cameo.

Make the Bail

19 Thread the needle through the pearl that is closest to the center at the top of the cameo. Pick up three 11° seed beads and pass the needle through the pearl and the first two 11°s to begin a RAW (figure 9).

figure 9

20 Right angle weave for nine rows. For the tenth row, pick up one 11° seed bead and thread the needle through the initial pearl. Pick up another 11° and thread the needle back through the last 11° in the completed RAW unit (figure 10).

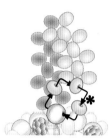

figure 19

21 Move the needle back through the starting pearl. Pick up one 15° and sew through the top of the next RAW unit in the opposite direction so the seed bead sits in the middle of the unit. Then pick up a pearl and sew through the top of the next RAW unit in the opposite direction so it sits in the middle of that unit (figure 11).

figure 11

22 Continue alternating a 15° and a pearl in each RAW stitch until reaching the end. Weave in the thread, tie half-hitch knots, and cut it off.

moonsHine necKLace

On occasion, when I start to get bored with a design, I like to try something totally new. So here I used free-form peyote stitch and mixed various leftover beads with seed beads. Then I spiced up the design by surrounding a druzy stone with the beadwork.

This pattern explores free-form peyote stitch in novel and exciting ways. When I completed the design, I felt like I had shaken things up a bit. The spice of life is what makes beading a passion. By working with this technique, I was able to delve deeply into understanding my process as an artist.

SUPPLIES

Bead Soup 1*, 15–20 g

Bead Soup 2**, 17 stones, 7–10 mm

48 silver size 8° seed beads

Size 11° seed beads, 1–2 g

FireLine 6 lb. test

Beading needles, size 12

Tape measure

* A variety of leftover sizes and colors: seed beads, 8° and 11°; round crystals, 2 mm; round pearls, 2 and 3 mm; Delicas, bugles, charlottes, peanut beads, super duos, etc.

** Stones, pearls, crystals, etc. Use all of the same kind of stone or a variety—irregular sizes are okay. I used oval-shaped pearls and druzy stones.

CLASP SUPPLIES

Silver size 11° seed beads, 1 g

Silver size 11° Delica beads, 1 g

4 silver size 15° seed beads

2 white pearls, 3 mm

DIMENSIONS

17½ inches (44.5 cm)

STITCHES

Free-form flat peyote stitch

Right angle weave (RAW)

Even-count flat peyote stitch

LEVEL

Intermediate

ROUND STONES

In choosing a center stone for each free-form unit, I found that a round shape was easier to use than any other. A round stone is simple to surround and lends itself well to blending with the free-form stitch.

Surround a Stone with Bead Soup

1 Thread a needle with one arm-length of thread, leaving a six-inch (15.2 cm) tail, and use a stopper bead. Dump the Bead Soup 1 mixture onto your work surface. Randomly string 1¾ inches (4.4 cm) of beads.

2 Stitch even-count flat peyote for five rows randomly using pieces you just strung. Don't cut the thread.

3 As shown in figure 1, pick up one of the stones in Bead Soup 2, line it up approximately one-quarter of the way into the stitch, and pierce through the beadwork. Sew through one of the beads in the peyote stitch, back through the stone, then pierce through the stitched beadwork close to the stone to reinforce it. Reinforce at least one more time (figure 1).

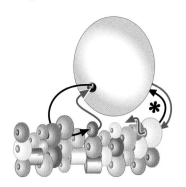

figure 1

4 Configure the stitched beadwork around the stone and sew the ends together to secure the stone (figure 2). Add beads by using free-form peyote as necessary to get the piece to lie in a ring around the stone without showing thread. Though, as I mentioned, this works best when the stone has a round shape, don't worry if this ring is not a perfect circle—that's the point of free-form design.

figure 2

5 Build a bridge (or several if needed) to fill any gap that has been left between the two ends of the beadwork ring. To do so, position your needle inside the ring and pierce outward through the beadwork. Pick up enough random pieces from Bead Soup 1 to connect to the other side. You can also use a few peyote stitches with a variety of beads to reinforce (figure 3).

figure 3

6 Thread the tail, weave it in, tie half-hitch knots, and cut it off. Leave the working threads hanging on each sur-rounded stone.

7 Follow steps 1–6 to create 17 separate units of a stone captured within a bead-work ring.

14 Pick up two 11°s and run your needle through two seed beads in the middle of one of the end stones. Pick up two 11°s and complete the RAW unit. Weave through the RAW unit to reinforce it, tying half-hitch knots along the way. End the thread.

Connect the Clasp's Toggle

15 Using the remaining thread on the toggle, weave to the center through two Delicas. Pick up six 11°s and go back through the two Delicas in the toggle, then four 11°s to make the first RAW unit.

16 Continue steps 13 and 14 until the chain is the same length as the one on the other end.

Connect the Surrounded Stones

8 Form the 17 stone units into a design that you find pleasing. For example, there may be certain stones that you prefer to position in the front of the piece.

9 Select a seed bead in the middle of the beadwork that surrounds one of the stone units and run your needle through it. Pick up three 8° seed beads, pass through a seed bead in the middle of the beadwork around an adjacent unit (figure 4, black thread path), and pass back through the three 8°s (figure 4, red thread path). Repeat the thread path several times to reinforce. Weave in the thread, tie half-hitch knots, and end it.

figure 4

10 Repeat step 9 until all 17 stone units are connected.

Make the Clasp

11 Follow the directions on page 19 to create a Standard Clasp. After completing the toggle and ring, leave the threads hanging.

Connect the Ring

12 Use the hanging thread on the ring portion of the clasp and weave to two center seed beads in the ditch. Pick up six 11°s and go back through the two seed beads on the clasp plus four 11°s to make the first RAW unit.

13 Pick up six 11°s and right angle weave. Continue to right angle weave until the chain reaches your desired length (I did five RAW units).

MIX IT UP
This design provides a great way to use some of the different leftovers in your stash that are "begging" for a home in one of your jewelry pieces. In addition, you can use druzy beads, pearls, glass beads, gemstones, or anything you like as the focal pieces. The sky is the limit—you can mix as much or as little as desired.

Don't be content with making only a necklace; you can also try a bracelet with this idea. Once you have your color palette, there is very little thinking involved. The beauty of free-form is that you can stitch without ever making a mistake!

chain reaction necklace

I often like to focus on a stitch and make a small beaded sample to determine whether an idea has the potential to become a "fine jewelry-like piece." I did that on this necklace, twisting and turning to create a fancy chain combining three different components that add depth to the piece.

SUPPLIES

Gold twin beads, 15 g

Gold size 11° seed beads, 9 g

Gold size 11° Delicas, 2 g

Gold size 15° seed beads, 0.5 g

250 to 280 crystal AB round crystals, 2 mm

24 dark blue pearls, 3 mm

24 crystal AB crystal bicones, 3 mm

2 crystal AB round crystals, 8mm

FireLine 6 lb. test

Beading needles, size 12

CLASP SUPPLIES

Gold size 11° seed beads 1 g

Gold size 11° Delica beads, 1g

Gold size 15° seed beads, 1g

2 dark blue pearls, 3 mm

DIMENSIONS

21 inches (53.3 cm)

STITCHES

Right angle weave (RAW)

Even-count tubular peyote stitch

LEVEL

Intermediate

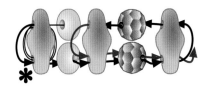

THE ADVANTAGE OF FLAT TWIN BEADS

Twin beads aren't uniform in size. Because I find the flatter ones to be a little more even, I chose them to create the links. So take the time to comb through them and pick out the ones that are flatter. This will make the beadwork look more uniform.

Sections of Links

1 Thread the needle with one arm-length of thread. Leaving a 6-inch (15.2 cm) tail, pick up one twin bead and run the needle through its holes twice in a circular motion to reinforce the stitch (figure 1).

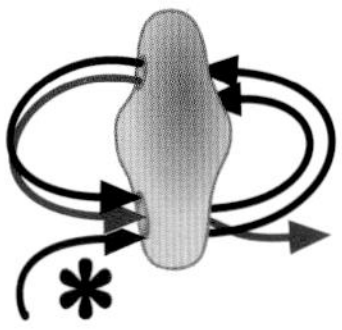

figure 1

2 Pick up one 11° and one twin bead. Run the needle through the 11° and one hole of the twin bead. Pass through the next twin bead hole (on the opposite side of the bead). Pick up one 11° and go back through the second hole of the first twin bead added (figure 2).

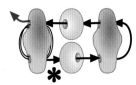

figure 2

3 Pass the needle through the starting twin bead hole, the 11°, and the next twin bead hole sewn through. Pick up one 2-mm crystal and one twin bead. Pass the needle through the next twin bead hole. Pick up one 2-mm crystal. Go through the twin bead at the start (in this case, the second twin bead). Go back through first twin bead hole in the row. Pass the needle through the crystal and the first hole of the next twin bead (figure 3).

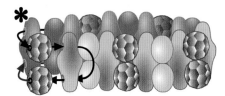

figure 3

4 Pick up one 11° and one twin bead. Go through the next twin bead hole. Pick up one 11°. Run the needle through the twin bead at the start (in this case the third twin bead). Go back through the first twin bead hole in the row. Pass through the 11° and the first hole of the next twin bead.

5 Continue in RAW until you've made 10 rows total.

6 Make a final row as follows. Pick up one 2-mm crystal and run the needle through the first twin bead hole of the first twin bead added. Go through the second twin bead hole. Pick up one 2-mm crystal. Put the needle through the second twin bead hole in the last twin bead added. Reinforce it. Weave in both the working thread and the tail, tie half-hitch knots, and cut it (figure 4). You've now completed one link.

figure 4

7 Make four more links, catching the previous link in each one before you close it, to make a section five links long. Then make five more sections each five links long, for a total of six sections containing five links each.

Beaded Cylinder

8 Thread the needle with one and a half arm-lengths of thread. Leaving a 12-inch (30.5 cm) tail, pick up eight 11°s and run the needle through the first two 11°s strung to create a unit. Move the needle through four more 11°s to put it in position for RAW (figure 5).

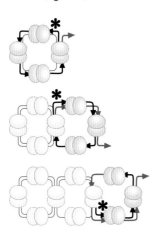

figure 5

9 RAW for six stitches total (eight beads per stitch).

10 Step up and do a second row of RAW (figure 6).

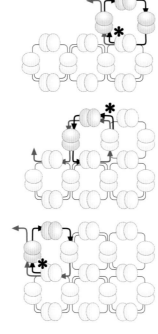

figure 6

11 Step up and do a third row of RAW.

12 For the fourth row, RAW rows 1 and 3 together. Pick up two 11°s and run the needle through the top two adjacent 11°s in row 1. Pick up two 11°s and pass the needle through the two adjacent 11°s in row 3. Weave the needle around the first unit created through the next top two 11°s in row 3. Pick up two 11°s and take the needle through the two 11°s in the next unit created in row 1.

Continue RAW (you will only be adding one side with two 11°s each time) until you reach the end (figure 7).

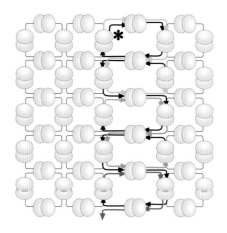

figure 7

13 Choose the closest row and put the needle through the bottom two 11°s in the first unit.

14 Pick up one 15°, one bicone, and one 15°. Sew to the opposite side of the unit in the opposite way. Pick up one 15°, one crystal pearl, and one 15°. Sew to the opposite side of the unit in the opposite direction (figure 8).

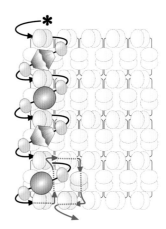

figure 8

15 Still referring to figure 8, alternate sewing a bicone and crystal pearl in each unit in the row. Then move the needle around the RAW following the stitch pattern to the next row.

92

16 Pick up one 15° one crystal pearl, and one 15°. Sew to the opposite side of the unit in the opposite direction. Pick up one 15°, one bicone, and one 15°. Sew to the opposite side of the unit in the opposite direction. Continue alternating until the row is completed (figure 9).

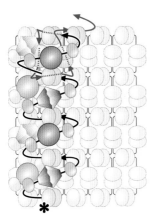

figure 9

17 Follow steps 14 and 15 for the next row.

18 Follow step 16 for the final row.

19 Pick up three 11°s and do a RAW stitch to start the strap. Continue doing a four-unit RAW unit until there are five units in total. Repeat on the opposite side of the cylinder.

20 Once the section of five links is ready on each side, pick up one 11° and sew back through the original 11° on the base. Pick up one 11° and sew through the final 11° at the top of the last unit (figure 10). Repeat, attaching the links on the opposite side to complete the strap. Weave in the threads on both sides, tie half-hitch knots, and cut them. Make two more beaded cylinders caught between sections of links, for a total of three.

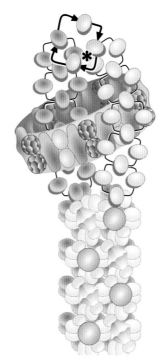

figure 10

Crystal Circles

21 Thread the needle with one arm-length of thread. Leaving a 6-inch (15.2 cm) tail, pick up 24 Delicas and pass your needle through the first three to make a circle.

22 Stitch even-count tubular peyote for five rows total. (Remember, the first two rows make three rows. Step up at the end of each row.) Weave in the tail, tie half-hitch knots, and cut it.

23 Move the working thread to the center of the peyote stitch. Pierce it through to the inside. Pick up one 8-mm crystal. Sew through the middle of the peyote stitch on the opposite side of the circle. Reinforce it one time (figure 11).

figure 11

24 Move the thread back to the top of one end of the circle. Move the needle down one Delica on the diagonal in the base. Stitch each ditch in the row with one 11° (figure 12).

figure 12

25 Still referring to figure 12, move the needle down one Delica on the diagonal in the base. Stitch each ditch in the row with one 11°.

26 For the third row, repeat step 25.

27 Orient the 8-mm crystal so the hole is horizontal. Find two 11°s in the middle row of ditches that line up the best with the hole on one side. Pick up six 11°s and create a RAW stitch of eight 11°s using the two 11°s in the middle of the base as two of the beads. Weave five more rows of RAW (figure 13).

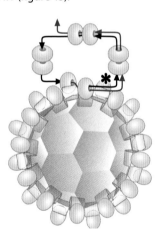

figure 13

28 Repeat step 27 on the opposite side.

29 Once the section of five links is complete, place the strap around the first link on the end. Pick up two 11°s and RAW into the first two 11°s in the base where you started. Pick up two 11°s and complete the RAW stitch. Weave in the thread, tie half-hitch knots and cut it off. Repeat step 21 on the opposite side of the same crystal circle (on both sides). Make two.

Clasp

30 Follow the directions on page 19 to create a Standard Clasp.

31 Move the remaining thread to a middle 11° in the ring portion of the clasp. Pick up three 11°s. RAW for five rows. For the sixth row, put the strap around the top link in the chain. Pick up one 11°, and put the needle through the original 11° in the base of the circle clasp. Pick up one 11°, and put the needle through the top of the last RAW unit completed. Weave in the thread, tie-half-hitch knots, and cut it off.

32 Move the needle to a center Delica in the toggle. Repeat step 31 for 12 rows total.

Assemble the Remaining Components

Attach the components in this order:
ring
one section of five links
one cylinder
one section of five links
one crystal circle
one section of five links
one cylinder
one section of five links
one crystal circle
one section of five links
one cylinder
one section of five links
toggle

SUPPLIES

Size 11° seed beads:
   Gold, 4 g (color A)
   White, 0.5 g (color B)

Gold size 15° seed beads, 1 g

30 dark blue crystal pearls, 3 mm

30 crystal AB crystal bicones, 3 mm

1 round tiger's-eye bead, 14–20 mm

1 silk cord necklace, 18 inches (45.7 cm)

FireLine 6 lb. test

Beading needles, size 12

DIMENSIONS

Beaded slide, 2½ inches (6.4 cm)

STITCH

Right angle weave (RAW)

LEVEL

Intermediate

FITTING YOUR SLIDE

If you have a particular necklace that you'd like to place the slide on, but you're not sure the slide will fit over its clasp, zip up the tube of RAW around the necklace, and then embellish the beadwork.

GIRLS' NIGHT OUT
necklace

Picture this: It's the end of an exhausting workweek, and soon you'll meet the girls for dinner to unwind and share some good gossip. The past few days have been long, and you're looking forward to seeing your friends, who are just as anxious as you to release life's pressures with a night out. Since you wouldn't have time to change clothes before going out, this morning you decided on a casually elegant look for the day and put on this necklace, which you created to perfectly match your favorite casual work outfit. It's such a great combination, and you've been getting compliments on the piece all day.

1 Thread the needle with one wingspan of thread. Leaving a 6-inch (15.2 cm) tail, pick up eight As and put the needle through the first two As strung to create a square unit. Move the needle through four more As to position it for RAW (figure 1).

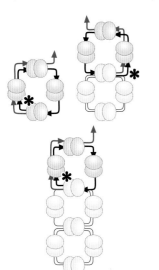

figure 1

2 Continue to refer to figure 1. Pick up six As. Put the needle through the top two As of the previous unit, then move the needle through four more As to position it at the side of the unit.

3 Repeat step 3 until you have 15 RAW units.

Note: The thread path will alternate with each stitch.

4 Position the needle so it's exiting from the top of the unit by moving it over two additional As from the end (figure1).

5 Referring to figure 2, pick up six As and RAW to begin the second row. For the next stitch and all following stitches in the row, pick up four As and RAW. Continue to RAW until you have five rows of 15 RAW units (figure 2).

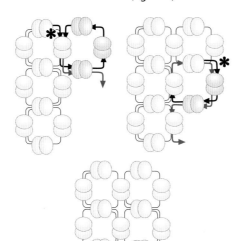

figure 2

6 Zip row 1 and row 5 together to create a sixth row. With the needle coming out of the first top unit on the fifth row, pick up two As and sew into the top unit in the first row. Pick up two As and sew into the top unit on the fifth row, then weave around the new RAW unit to the second unit down on the fifth row. Continue adding pairs of As and alternating the needle placement until all 15 rows are zipped together (figure 3). Once the zipping is completed, run the thread through the last unit completed to reinforce. Leave the thread in place.

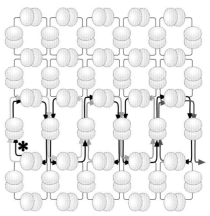

figure 3

7 Move the needle to a unit on one end of the piece with the thread facing inside toward the beadwork.

8 Follow along with figure 4. Pick up one 15°, one B, and one 15°. Put the needle through the top of the next unit in the opposite direction so the B sits in the hole. Repeat, substituting one 3-mm bicone for the B. Repeat, substituting one 3-mm pearl for the B. Repeat this pattern until you reach the end of the row (15 stitches in total)

9 Weave the needle through the beadwork until it's sitting at the end of the next row (the end you wound up on). Fill in the rows as follows, always putting a 15° on either end of the bead in the pattern. Once you reach the end of each row, weave the needle through the beadwork to position it at the end of the next row (figures 4 and 5).

Row Two	Row Three	Row Four	Row Five	Row Six
One B	One pearl	One pearl	One bicone	One bicone
One pearl	One B	One bicone	One pearl	One B
One bicone	One bicone	One B	One B	One pearl

10 Weave the needle to the center of the beadwork, between two As in the center of the slide. Pick up three As, the tiger's-eye bead, and one A. Sew back through the tiger's-eye, the three As and back through the base (figure 6). Weave in the tail, tie half-hitch knots, and end the thread. Slide the pendant over the silk cord to wear it.

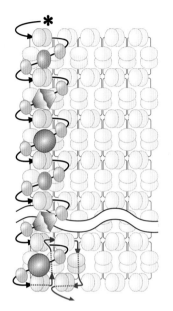

figure 4

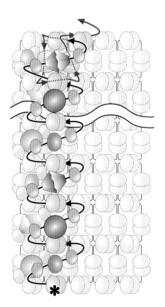

figure 5

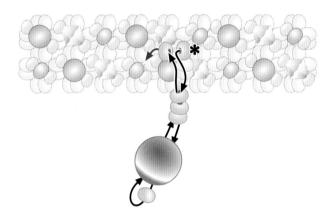

figure 6

Variation

DAISY DARLING NECKLACE

While designing this necklace, I focused on one idea: "What would I wear if I were invited to an elegant party hosted by someone wealthy or famous?" I would want a piece with pearls and diamonds (okay, crystals) to showcase my eveningwear. With this in mind, I created a three-component necklace that I thought would stand out with an elite crowd.

SUPPLIES

Size 11° seed beads:
  One shade of Gold, 8.5 g (color A)
  A second shade of Gold, 0.5 g (color B)

Gold size 11° Delicas, 8.5 g

Gold size 15° seed beads, 3.5 g

4 tanzanite AB 2X round crystals, 6 mm

12 peridot AB 2X crystal bicones, 4 mm

100 crystal AB round crystals, 2 mm

2 white crystal pearls, 10 mm

28 white crystal pearls, 3 mm

FireLine 6 lb. test

Beading needles, size 12

CLASP SUPPLIES

Gold size 11° seed beads, 1 g

Gold size 11° Delicas, 1 g

Gold size 15° seed beads, 1 g

2 white pearls, 3 mm

7 crystal AB round crystals, 2 mm

DIMENSIONS

20½ inches (52.1 cm)

STITCHES

Even-count tubular peyote stitch

Right angle weave (RAW)

Fringe stitch

LEVEL

Advanced

Make the Components

Component 1

1 Thread the needle with one wingspan of thread. Leaving a 6-inch (15.2 cm) tail, pick up 24 Delicas and put the needle through the first three to make a ring.

2 Stitch even-count tubular peyote with Delicas for five rows. (Remember, the first two rows make three rows.) Remember to step up at the end of each row. Thread the tail, weave it in, tie half-hitch knots, and end it.

3 Go back to the working thread and position it in the first ditch in the circle by moving the needle down one Delica on the diagonal in the base.

Note: Figures 1 and 2 are shown flat for simplicity although the piece itself is actually round.

4 Tie a half-hitch knot. Stitch in each ditch with one A bead. Continue stitching in all the ditches in this row with one A bead. Do not step up after the last stitch (figure 1).

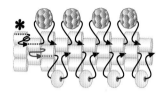

figure 1

5 Still referring to figure 1, move the needle down one Delica bead on the diagonal. Stitch in each ditch with one A bead. Continue stitching in all the ditches in this row with one A bead. Don't step up after the last stitch.

6 Repeat step 5.

7 Weave the needle through the piece up to the first row of A beads (the middle row). Put the needle through one A in that row to start.

8 Pick up two 15°s, one 2-mm crystal, and two 15°s. Sew through the next A on the base. Pick up two 15°s, one B, and two 15°s. Sew through the next A in the base. Repeat this alternating pattern all the way around (figure 2).

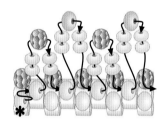

figure 2

9 Move the needle down to the bottom row of A beads in the base. Put the needle through one A in that row to start. Pick up two 15°s, one 2-mm crystal, and two 15°s. Sew through the next A in the base. Pick up two 15°s, one A, and two 15°s. Sew through the next A in the base. Pick up one 15°, one 4-mm bicone, and one 15°. Sew back through the bicone to make a fringe stitch. Pick up one 15° and sew through the next A in the base. Repeat the pattern all the way around (figure 3). You have completed one Component 1; leave the remaining thread in place. Make two more, for a total of three.

figure 3

Component 2

10 Thread the needle with one and a half arm-lengths of thread and leave a 6-inch (15.2 cm) tail. Pick up 26 Delicas and put the needle through the first three strung to make a ring.

11 Stitch five rows of even-count tubular peyote, keeping a medium tension. (Remember, the first two rows make three rows.) Remember to step up at the end of each row. Thread the tail, weave it in, tie half-hitch knots, and end it.

12 Weave the needle to the middle of the Delica beads and pierce through so that it's inside the ring. Pick up one 10-mm pearl and sew through to the opposite side of the Delicas. Weave the needle around so it can be repositioned to go through the same Delica, then pierce it back through to the center of the piece. Sew through the pearl again to reinforce it (figure 4).

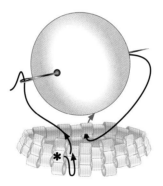

figure 4

13 Move the needle to the first row of ditches. Stitch in each ditch with A beads all the way around.

14 Move the needle down one Delica bead on the diagonal. Stitch in each ditch with A beads. Continue stitching in all the ditches in this row with A beads. Don't step up after the last stitch.

15 Weave the needle through an A on the last row of ditches completed (this becomes your top row). Pick up two 15°s, one 2-mm round, and two 15°s. Sew through the next A in the row. Repeat this pattern all the way around (figure 5). You have completed one Component 2; leave the remaining thread in place. Make one more, for a total of two.

figure 5

Component 3

16 Thread the needle with one and a half arm-lengths of thread and leave a 6-inch (15.2 cm) tail. Pick up 20 Delicas and put the needle through the first three strung to make a ring.

17 Stitch five rows of even-count tubular peyote, keeping a medium tension. (Remember, the first two rows make three rows.) Remember to step up at the end of each row. Thread the tail, weave it in, tie half-hitch knots, and end it.

18 Weave the needle to the top row of ditches. Stitch in each ditch with A beads until reaching the end of the row.

19 Move the needle down one Delica on the diagonal. Stitch in each ditch with A beads. Continue stitching in all the ditches in this row with A beads. Don't step up after the last stitch. Repeat for the final row of ditches.

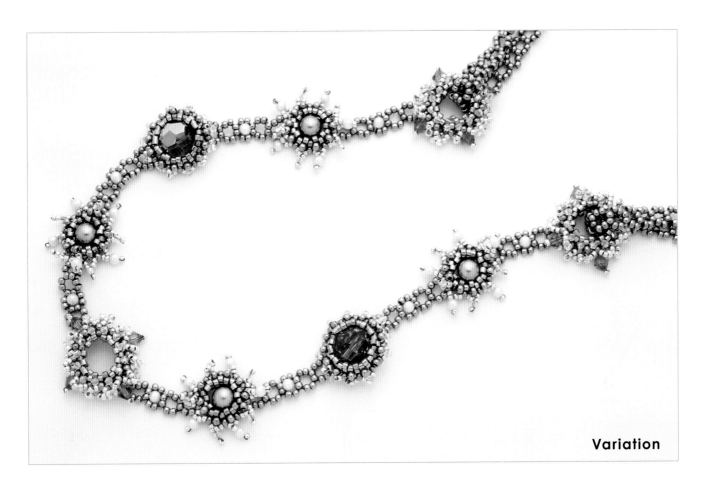

Variation

20 Weave the needle through a top "up" Delica bead. Pick up a 6-mm round crystal and stitch through a top "up" Delica directly across on the opposite side, putting the needle in through the Delica the opposite way. Reinforce it by putting the needle back through the 6-mm round and the starting "up" Delica on the opposite side.

21 Weave the needle through an A on the last row of ditches completed. Pick up two 15°s, one 3-mm pearl, and one 15°. Put the needle back through the pearl. Pick up two 15°s. Sew through the next A in the row. Pick up two 15°s, one 2-mm round crystal, and one 15°. Put the needle back through the 2-mm round. Pick up two 15°s. Sew through the next A in the row.

Repeat the pattern all the way around (figure 6). You've completed one Component 3; leave the remaining thread in place. Make three more, for a total of four.

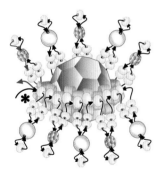

figure 6

Connect the Components

Note: Before stitching the components together, make sure they line up straight and face forward.

Connect Component 1 to Component 3

22 Thread the needle onto the excess thread on Component 3. Weave the needle so it's coming out through the top two A beads closest to a 4-mm bicone. The two A beads will be the start of the first RAW stitch.

23 Pick up six A beads and make the first RAW square, including the two A beads on Component 3 in the base. Continue picking up six A beads and make three more units (four units total of RAW).

24 For the last RAW unit, pick up two A beads and sew through two existing A beads in the middle row of Component 1. Pick up two more A beads and complete the RAW stitch.

25 Weave back through the RAW and tie half-hitch knots. When you reach the third unit, pick up one 3-mm pearl and sew it into the opposite end of the RAW square diagonally. Continue weaving in the thread and tying half-hitch knots (figure 7). Cut the thread to end it.

figure 7

Connect Component 3 to Component 2

26 Thread the needle onto the excess thread from component 3. Line it up so it's on the opposite side (connect it in a straight line).

27 Put the needle through two A beads in the middle row.

28 Use the two A beads in the base as the start of the RAW stitch. Repeat step 23 for three more units.

29 For the last row of RAW, pick up two A beads and sew through two existing A beads in the middle row of Component 2.

30 Repeat step 25.

31 Continue to connect all of the components in the following order:
Component 1
Component 3
Component 2
Component 3
Component 1
Component 3
Component 2
Component 3
Component 1

Side Straps

32 Thread the needle with two arm-lengths of thread. Leaving a 6-inch (15.2 cm) tail, pick up eight A beads and put the needle through the first two added to make a circle. Put the needle through four more A beads to position it for RAW. Stitch a RAW strap 7 inches (17.8 cm) long.

33 Repeat step 32 to make a second strap. Both straps must be the same length.

34 Put one strap through Component 1 on an end. RAW the first and last square together so that it makes a chain around Component 1 (figure 8). Repeat on the opposite side.

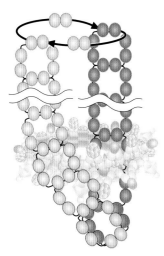

figure 8

Clasp

35 Follow the directions for the Standard Clasp on page 19.

Attach the Toggle

36 Thread the needle onto the excess thread on the strap. Position the needle so it's exiting from the middle of two RAW units. Pick up eight A beads and sew into one Delica in the middle of the toggle. Pick up eight A beads and sew into the opposite side of the RAW unit. Reinforce it several times. Weave in the tail, tie half-hitch knots, and end the thread.

Attach the Ring

37 Thread the needle onto the excess thread on the other strap. Position the needle so it's exiting from the middle of two RAW units. Pick up five A beads and sew into two adjacent A beads on the circle. Pick up five A beads and sew into the opposite side of the RAW unit. Reinforce it several times. Weave in the tail, tie half-hitch knots, and end the thread.

reflections pendant

Not every piece that looks like fine jewelry has to take hours to make. I love creating lavish necklaces, but when I'm not in the mood to stitch for hours, a pendant is a good substitute. You can get a very romantic look with a small, simple piece.

Gold size 11° seed beads, 2 g

Gold size 15° seed beads, 0.5 g

Gold-plated size 15° Czech charlottes, 0.2 g

1 clear foiled faceted crystal rectangle, 25 x 16 mm

11 pale pink pearls, 3 mm

11 crystal AB crystal bicones, 3 mm

20 crystal AB round crystals, 2 mm

FireLine 6 lb. test

Beading needles, size 12 and 13

DIMENSIONS

2 x 1⅛ inches (5.1 x 2.8 cm), including bail

STITCHES

Right angle weave (RAW)

Even-count tubular peyote stitch

Fringe stitch

LEVEL

Advanced

WHERE TO START

Because the top and bottom rows of right angle weave in this design both contain a smaller seed bead in each stitch, I decided to start beading at the center row, which consists of all 11°s. So keep in mind that you work the center row first, and then create the top and bottom rows.

Capture the Crystal Faceted Rectangle

1 Thread the needle with one wingspan of thread. Leaving a 6-inch (15.2 cm) tail, pick up four 11°s. Put the needle through all four 11°s to make a ring. Position the needle for RAW by moving it through three more 11°s to put it on the opposite end of the unit from the tail.

2 Pick up three 11°s and RAW. Repeat until you have 21 units total.

3 Move the needle to the top of the end unit. Pick up one 11°, one 15°, and one 11° and stitch one RAW unit. The needle should be coming out of an 11° on the left side of the first RAW unit in the second row (figure 1).

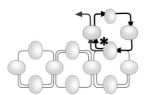

figure 1

4 Pick up one 15° and one 11°. Put the needle through the bottom 11° (from the first row), through the side 11° (the previous unit), through the 15° and 11° just added, and the bottom 11° on the unit below (figure 2).

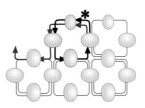

figure 2

5 Pick up one 11° and one 15°. Put the needle through the side of the previous unit, through the bottom 11°, and the 11° just added (figure 3).

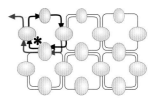

figure 3

Note: You will want all of the 15°s on the top of the row.

6 Repeat steps 4 and 5 until all 21 units are complete.

7 Move the needle to the bottom of the RAW strip (the opposite side). Repeat step 3 once. Repeat steps 4 and 5 until all 21 units are complete. Weave in the tail, tie half-hitch knots, and end it (figure 4).

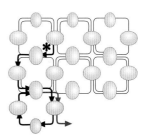

figure 4

8 Connect the ends of the strip into a ring by positioning the needle so it's exiting from one side 11° on an end unit at the top, then pick up one 15° and sew through the 11° on the opposite side of the strip. Pick up one 11° and sew through the side 11° (at your starting point). Put the needle through the top 15°, side 11°, and bottom 11°, then side 11° of the middle row. Pick up one 11° to complete the next unit. Move the needle through the RAW unit once again until it is positioned at the bottom of the connection. Pick up one 15° and complete the final RAW unit by sewing through all of the beads in the unit (figure 5). Place the crystal rectangle inside the beadwork.

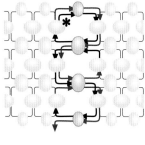

figure 5

9 Position the needle so it's exiting from a top 15° in the unit. Pick up one 15° charlotte. Stitch even-count peyote for one row (you do not have to step up), using 15° charlottes. Move the needle down through the beadwork to one of the very bottom 15°s and repeat to add 15° charlottes along that edge (figure 6).

Note: I have size 13 needles on hand to work with 15° charlottes if necessary. Also, if you need to tighten the rectangle a bit, add a second row of charlottes to the front side.

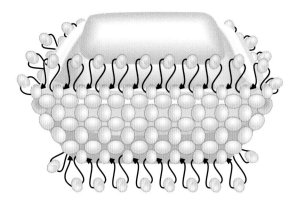

figure 6

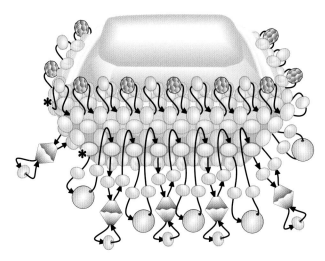

figure 7

Embellish

Refer to figure 7 for steps 7 through 14.

10 Position the needle so it's exiting from the top 11° facing sideways (middle of the first RAW row with 11°s). Pick up one 15° and stitch across to the next 11° in the RAW unit. Pick up one 2-mm crystal and stitch across to the next 11° in the RAW unit. Repeat the pattern until the row is completed.

11 Move the needle down to the next RAW unit so it's exiting from an 11° facing sideways.

12 Pick up one 15°, one crystal pearl, and one 15°. Stitch across to the next 11° in the RAW unit.

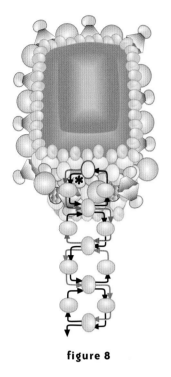

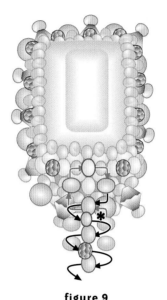

figure 8

figure 9

13 Pick up one 15°, one bicone, and one 15°. Put the needle back through the bicone. Pick up one 15°. Stitch across to the next 11° in the RAW unit.

Note: The pearls should be below the 2-mm crystals and the bicones below the 15°s in the row above it.

14 Repeat steps 12 and 13 until the row is complete.

Add the Bail

15 Move the needle to the middle 11° at the back of one of the shorter ends of the beadwork. Pick up three 11°s and stitch a RAW unit. Right angle weave for 11 units.

For the 12th unit, attach the strip to the front with a RAW stitch, forming the bail (figure 8). Embellish the bail as follows; with the needle positioned through the bottom 11° on the last unit, pick up one 15° and sew through the top 11° on the next unit in the opposite way. Pick up one 2-mm crystal. Sew through the top on the next unit in the opposite way.

16 Continue alternating the pattern until you reach the end of the bail (figure 9). Weave in the thread, tie half-hitch knots, and end it.

Back

Designer envy necklace

I love the work of today's classic designers. Many of them create elegant looks by using some very basic pieces that are cleverly put together. I've spent many hours in high-end jewelry and department stores just browsing these creations. My eye seems most drawn to the pieces that mix metals, pearls, and splashes of diamonds. To honor this style, I mixed high-quality metal seed beads with crystals and pearls to achieve a very wearable yet noticeable design.

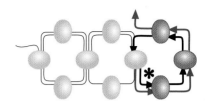

CONQUERING TUBULAR RIGHT ANGLE WEAVE

People seem to think tubular right angle weave is really challenging to stitch, but it's not hard to follow if you think in terms of numbers. Once you start stitching in the round, remember that in each row, three 11°s make up the first unit, two 11°s make up the second unit as well as the third unit, and one 11° makes up the final unit. Always remember that right angle weave creates a square unit and not a circle unit. It looks circular due to the shape of the beads, but the stitch actually gives you an evenly distributed four-sided shape.

Links

Tubular RAW from a Flat RAW Start

1 Thread the needle with one wingspan of thread. Leaving a 10-inch (25.4 cm) tail, pick up four 11° seed beads. Move the needle over two additional 11°s to put it in place for the next RAW stitch (figure 1).

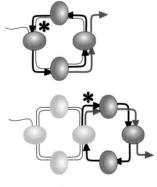

figure 1

2 Pick up three 11° seed beads and do a RAW stitch.

3 Pick up three more 11°s and do a RAW stitch. Move the needle to the top of the last square of RAW completed (figure 2).

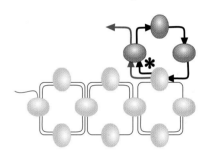

figure 2

4 Pick up three more 11° seed beads and create one more RAW unit at the start of the second row (figure 3).

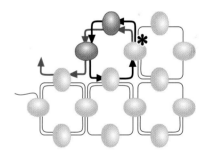

figure 3

5 Stitch two more RAW units in row 2 (figures 4 and 5).

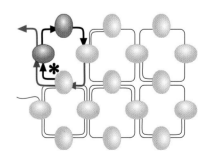

figure 4

figure 5

6 Move the needle to the side of the last unit of RAW. Pick up one 11° seed bead and sew through the side of the first RAW unit in row 2. Pick up one 11° and sew through the side of the last RAW unit in row 2 (figure 6).

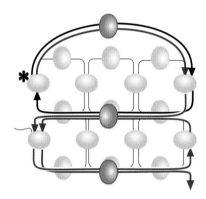

figure 6

7 Still referring to figure 6, move the needle through the top, the side, and the bottom of the third RAW unit in row 2, then the side of the first RAW unit in row 1. Pick up one 11° seed bead and sew through the RAW in a square to close up the tube. This should result in a two-square tube of four RAW stitches total all the way around.

Tubular RAW

Refer to figure 7 for steps 8 through 12.

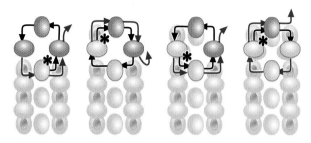

figure 7

8 Position the needle so it's exiting from one top 11° seed bead in the tube. Pick up three 11° seed beads and do a RAW stitch.

9 With the needle coming out of the first 11° added in the last step, pick up two 11°s and do one RAW stitch.

10 With the needle coming out of the top of the unit of the previous row, pick up two 11°s and do one RAW stitch.

11 With the needle coming out of the side of the previous RAW unit, pick up one 11° seed bead. Put the needle through the side of the first RAW unit, then down through the top of the previous unit, through the side of the next unit, and finally through the top of the current unit.

12 Repeat steps 8 through 11 until the tube measures 2 inches (5.1 cm) long.

Close Up the Tube Circularly

Note: Close up the inside of the tube first.

13 With the needle coming out of a top 11° in the last unit, pick up one 11°. Find the top 11° on the opposite side of the tube that matches the inside position of the unit. Pick up one 11° and complete a RAW stitch, sewing the inside of the tube together (figure 8).

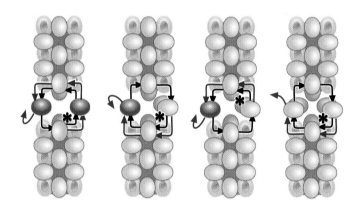

figure 8

14 Move the needle to the side of the next unit by going through the top 11° of the next unit. Pick up one 11° and RAW through the top of the opposite unit, the side of the new unit, and the 11° in the starting unit.

15 Pick up one 11° seed bead and repeat step 14.

Note: The stitching will be going in the opposite way.

16 For the last stitch, RAW the four touching sides of the unit together without adding any 11°s. Reinforce it once. Weave in the threads, tie half-hitch knots and end them.

Repeat steps 1 to 15 fourteen more times to make 15 links total.

Link Connectors

17 Thread the needle with one and a half arm-lengths of thread. Leaving an 8-inch (20.3 cm) tail, pick up three Delicas. Square stitch to create 10 rows three Delicas wide.

18 Note how rose montees have two channels in the back. With the needle coming out of the top of one side of the square stitch, sew through one rose montee by passing through just one channel, then sew through the second channel. Put the needle back through the first row of square stitch on the opposite side. Reinforce it once (figure 9).

figure 9

19 Weave the needle back through the rose montee. With the needle coming out of one of the channels, pick up three Delicas and pass the needle through the other channel.

20 Weave the needle back through the last completed row of square stitch, one channel in the rose montee, and the three Delicas just added (figure 10).

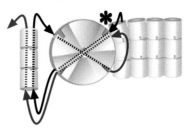

figure 10

21 Square stitch until there are 10 more rows of three Delicas across (figure 11).

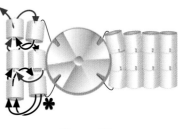

figure 11

22 With the needle coming out of the top of one side of the square stitch, sew through one channel in a rose montee, then through the second channel. Put the needle back through the first row of square stitch on the opposite side. Reinforce it once (figure 12). Weave back into the square stitch, tie half-hitch knots, and cut the thread. Thread the tail.

figure 12

23 As shown in figure 13, catch two links in the strip of beadwork and close the strip so it becomes a link connector by weaving the needle back through the square stitch on the opposite side and the rose montees several times (figure 13). Weave in the thread, tie half-hitch knots, and cut the thread.

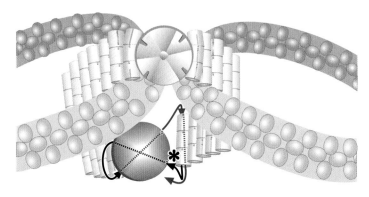

figure 13

24 Make another link connector and use it to connect one of the links connected in the previous step to a second link. Repeat 12 more times to form a chain consisting of the 15 links held together by 14 link connectors.

Clasp

25 Follow the directions for the standard clasp on page 19.

Attach the Toggle

26 Position the thread in the center of the toggle between two Delicas. Using two existing Delicas as the base for the RAW stitch, pick up six 11° seed beads. Go back through the starting two Delicas and four 11° seed beads to complete the first unit.

27 Pick up six more 11° seed beads and RAW. Repeat.

28 Pick up two 11° seed beads. Put the needle through two 11°s in the top of the middle of the link at either end of the chain. Complete the RAW unit. Weave the thread in through the RAW, tie half-hitch knots, and cut it.

Attach the Ring

29 Put the needle through two middle 15°s in the ditches. Pick up six 11° seed beads and do a RAW stitch.

30 Pick up six more 11°s and RAW. Repeat.

31 Pick up two 11°s. Put the needle through two 11°s in the top of the middle of the link at the other end of the chain. Complete the RAW stitch. Weave the thread in through the RAW, tie half-hitch knots, and cut it.

Rectangular Dangle

32 Thread the needle with two arm-lengths of thread. Leaving a 6-inch (15.2 cm) tail, pick up four 11° seed beads. Pass the needle through all four 11°s to make a unit. Position the needle for RAW by moving through two more 11°s to put it on the opposite end of the unit from the tail.

33 Pick up three 11° seed beads (to make the left side, top and right side of the square). Run the needle through the top 11° in the previous unit to make the next RAW stitch. Move the needle through two 11°s to position it to create the next unit.

34 Make 17 units total by following step 33.

35 Move the needle to the top of the side unit. Pick up one 11°, one 15° seed bead, and one 11°. Do a RAW stitch. The needle should be coming out of one 11° on the right side of the first RAW unit in the second row (figure 14).

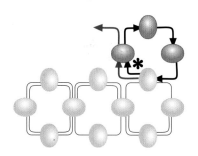

figure 14

36 Pick up one 15° seed bead and one 11°. Put the needle through the bottom 11° (from the first row), through the side 11° (the previous unit), through the 15° seed bead and 11° just added, and the bottom 11° of the unit below.

37 Repeat steps 35 and 36 until the row is completed.

38 As shown in figure 15, move the needle to the bottom of the RAW strip (opposite side). Repeat step 32.

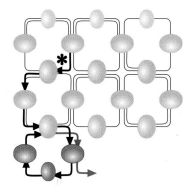

figure 15

39 Repeat steps 35 and 36 until the rows are complete. Weave in the tail, tie half-hitch knots, and cut it.

40 Referring to figure 16. Connect the ends of the strip into a ring by positioning the needle so it's exiting from one side 11° on an end unit at the top, then pick up one 15° and sew through the 11° on the opposite side of the strip. Pick up one 11° and sew through the side 11° (at your starting point). Put the needle through the top 15°, side 11°, and bottom 11°, then side 11° of the middle row. Pick up one 11° to complete the next unit. Move the needle through the RAW unit once again until it is positioned at the bottom of the connection. Pick up one 15° and complete the final RAW unit by sewing through all of the beads in the unit.

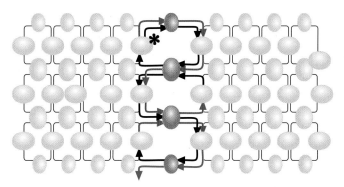

figure 16

41 Put the rectangular crystal inside the RAW strip. Position the needle so that it's coming out of a top 15° seed bead. Pick up one 15° charlotte and peyote stitch through the next 15°. Repeat until you reach the end. You do not have to step up. Weave the needle to the top 15°seed bead on the opposite side. Repeat to add a row of charlottes on the back side.

Note: I have size 13 needles on hand to work with the charlottes if necessary. If you need to tighten up the rectangle a bit, add a second row of charlottes to the front side (figure 17).

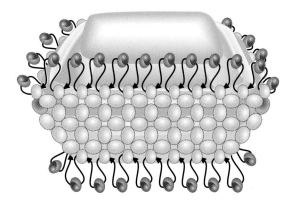

figure 17

42 Weave the needle to the upper 11°. Pick up one 2-mm crystal and stitch into the next side 11° in the opposite way. Pick up one 11° and stitch into the next 11° in the opposite way. Repeat this pattern all the way around (figure 18).

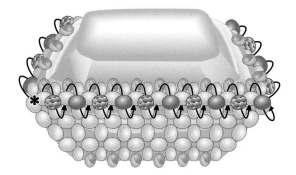

figure 18

43 In this step, you'll make a strap. Weave the needle to the top of the shorter side of the rectangle. Put the needle through the middle two 11°s in the second row. Pick up six 11°s and RAW. Do six more RAW stitches (figure 19).

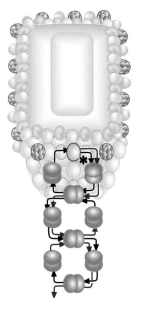

figure 19

44 Put the strap around the eighth link in the chain and attach it in the same place on the rectangle (same as the start) by making one last RAW stitch (figure 20).

figure 20

Pearl Dangles

45 Thread the needle with one and a half arm-lengths of thread. Leaving a 6-inch (15.2 cm) tail, pick up 32 Delicas Pass the needle through the first three to make a ring.

46 Stitch even-count tubular peyote with Delicas for five rows (the first two rows make three rows), remembering to step up after each row.

Note: If you stitch tightly, you may have to add two more Delicas to the circle; loose stitches may need two less Delicas.

47 Move the needle to the middle row, positioning it so it's inside the circle. Pick up one 12-mm pearl, string it on the thread, and sew through to the opposite side. Sew through the peyote and the pearl again to reinforce it. Move the needle to the top of one end. Thread the tail, weave it in, tie half-hitch knots, and cut it.

48 Go back to the working thread. Move the needle down one Delica bead on the diagonal. Tie a half-hitch knot. Stitch in the ditch with one 2-mm round crystal. Stitch in the next ditch with one 11°. Alternate the pattern all the way around the top row.

49 Move the needle down one Delica bead on the diagonal. Stitch in the ditch with 11°s all the way around.

50 Move the needle down one Delica bead on the diagonal. Repeat step 49.

51 Weave the needle through a top 11° (out of the ditch) in the middle row. Pick up three 11°s and do a RAW stitch. Continue in RAW stitch for seven rows (figure 21).

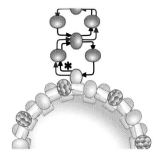

figure 21

52 Position the dangle in the sixth link on the chain. Make sure the dangles are facing the same way as the rectangle.

53 Create a RAW strap as described in steps 43 and 44, starting in the middle row. Reinforce it. Weave in the thread, tie half-hitch knots and cut it.

54 Make a second pearl dangle and hang it from the 10th link in the chain.

Crystal Dangles

55 Pick up 26 Delicas and put the needle through the first three to make a circle.

56 Stitch even-count tubular peyote with Delicas for five rows (the first two rows make three rows), remembering to step up after each row.

57 Pick up one 10-mm crystal, string it on the thread, and sew through to the opposite side. Sew through the peyote and the crystal again to reinforce it. Move the needle to the top of one end. Thread the tail, weave it in, tie half-hitch knots, and cut it.

58 Go back to the working thread. Move the needle down one Delica on the diagonal. Tie a half-hitch knot. Stitch in the ditch with one 11°. Repeat in each ditch until reaching the end of the row.

59 Move the needle down one Delica bead on the diagonal. Stitch in each ditch in the second row with one 11°. Repeat for the third row. Once completed, weave the needle through an 11° in the middle row. Pick up three 11°s and do a RAW stitch. Continue in RAW stitch for seven rows. Position the dangle in the fourth link on the chain, making sure it will hang from the same side of the chain as the rectangular dangle does. Do one RAW stitch in the same place as the start on the back of the dangle. Reinforce it.

60 Make a second crystal dangle and hang it from the 12th link in the chain.

SUPPLIES

Gold size 11° seed beads, 15 g

Gold size 11° Delicas, 6 g

Gold size 15° seed beads, 1 g

Gold size 1 bugle beads, 3.5 g

150 crystal AB round crystals, 2 mm

1 white pearl, 14 mm

2 round crystal pearls, 3 mm

Stopper bead

FireLine 6 lb. test

Beading needles, size 12

Bead mat

Reading glasses

Magnifier

Tape measure

DIMENSIONS

17 inches (43.2 cm)

STITCHES

Tubular right angle weave (Tubular RAW)

Even-count tubular peyote stitch

Right angle ladder stitch

LEVEL

Advanced

TIPS & TRICKS

In making all of the pieces for this necklace, the count is the key. Make sure that your counts are the same all the way around. I find it easiest to work on a relatively complex piece when interruptions are few and far between. Mental focus will definitely be your friend in completing this creation.

carousel necklace

I love working with circular patterns and have used a number of standard stitches to do so. For this necklace, I wanted to use a combined stitch I developed: right angle ladderstitch.

Designing for me is a piece-by-piece process—and like a puzzle, the pieces have to fit. I needed to solve a number of challenges to get the look I envisioned, including how to get the tube look. After making several trial-and-error pieces, I was able to determine what I needed, which included adding tubular RAW to the mix. Don't be afraid to try doing things in different ways when designing. Even if it takes a long time, the results are often worth it.

The Rope

1 To begin tubular RAW for the rope, thread the needle with one wingspan of thread, leaving a six-inch (15.2 cm) tail.

2 Pick up four 11° seed beads to make a RAW unit. Move the needle over two 11°s to put it in place for the next RAW unit (figure 1, top).

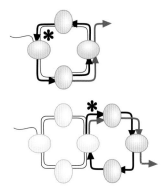

figure 1

3 Pick up three more 11° seed beads and run the needle through the first bead of the previous unit. Move the needle over two 11°s to put it in place for the next RAW unit (figure 1, bottom).

4 Pick up three additional 11° seed beads and make another RAW unit. Move the needle to the top of that unit (figure 2).

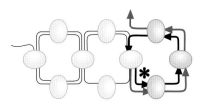

figure 2

5 Pick up three more 11°s and create one more RAW unit at the start of the second row (figure 3).

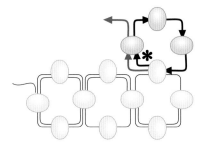

figure 3

6 Move the needle to the side of the last unit and pick up two more 11° seed beads. Sew through the top of the second unit in row 1 and the side of the first unit of row 2. Then move the needle through two 11°s. Move the needle through the top 11° of the first unit in row 1 (figure 4).

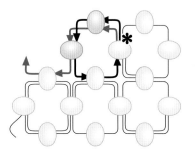

figure 4

7 Pick up two more 11° seed beads and continue with RAW, sewing through the adjacent bead in the previous unit and again through the top 11° of the first unit in row 1 (figure 5).

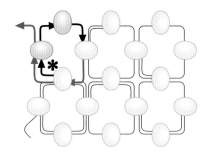

figure 5

8 Move the needle through the top, the side, and the bottom of the third RAW unit in row 2, then the outside bead of the first RAW unit in row 1. Pick up one 11° and sew through the side 11° in the third unit in row 1. Pick up another 11° and RAW in a square to close up the tube. Move through the next three 11°s in the new RAW unit. Sew through the end bead in the third unit in row 2. Pick up one 11° and sew through the end bead in the first unit in row 2. Then sew through the top bead in the last RAW unit formed. This should result in a two-square tube of four RAW stitches total all the way around (figure 6).

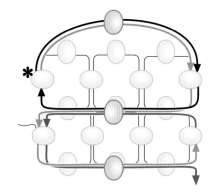

figure 6

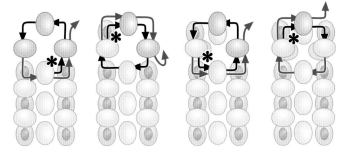

figure 7

Note: Refer to figure 7 for steps 9 through 12.

9 Position the needle so it's exiting from one top 11° in the tube. Pick up three 11°s and do a RAW stitch.

10 With the needle coming out of the side of the 11° of the first added, pick up two 11°s and do one RAW stitch.

11 With the needle coming out of the top of the unit of the previous row, pick up two 11°s and do one RAW stitch.

12 With the needle coming out of the side of the previous RAW unit, pick up one 11°. Put the needle through the side of the first RAW unit, then through the top of the previous unit, through the side of the next unit, and finally through the top of the current unit. Continue even-count tubular peyote stitch until the chain is approximately 16¹⁄₂ inches (41.9 cm) long, or a length of your preference. Once completed, leave the thread in place.

The Tube

Front: Square One

13 Thread the needle onto one wingspan of thread, leaving a 6-inch (15.2 cm) tail. Using right angle ladder stitch, pick up two bugle beads and ladder stitch them together so they lie side by side. Position the needle as shown (figure 8).

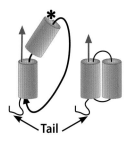

figure 8

14 Pick up one Delica, one 2-mm round crystal, and one Delica (this pattern is Group 1). Using the same thread, pick up two more bugle beads and ladder stitch them together so they align with the two bugles on the opposite side (figure 9).

figure 9

15 Pick up another Group 1. Stitch through the corresponding bugle on the opposite side as illustrated in figure 10 to complete the top of the first unit of the tube. Ladder down through the adjacent bugle without adding any beads (figure 10).

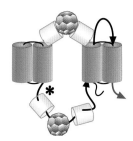

figure 10

Back: Square One

16 With the needle positioned as illustrated in figure 11, pick up one Delica, one 11° seed bead, and one Delica (this pattern is Group 2). Stitch through the next back bugle on the opposite side where the thread is coming out. Pick up another Group 2. Stitch through the next bugle (figure 11).

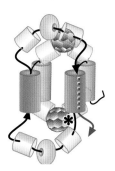

figure 11

17 With the needle coming out of the same bugle as the start of step 16, move it through the next Group 2 and the next bugle bead. Ladder down through the adjacent bugle to the front without adding any beads to get into position for the next unit (figure 12).

figure 12

Additional Square Units in the Base Row (Row 1)

18 Flip the beadwork over to the front, and pick up Group 1. Pick up two bugles and ladder stitch them together so they lie side by side (figure 13).

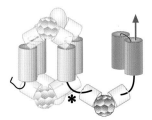

figure 13

19 Pick up Group 1 and sew through the front bugle of the first unit. Ladder through the adjacent bugle without adding any beads (figure 14).

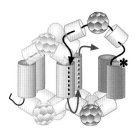

figure 14

20 Flip the beadwork again to the back. Pick up a Group 2 and sew through the next bugle. Pick up another Group 2 and sew through the first bugle (figure 15).

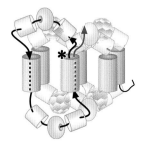

figure 15

21 Sew again through Group 2 and the next bugle, and ladder through the adjacent bugle without adding any beads (figure 16).

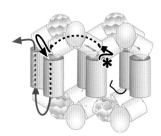

figure 16

Repeat steps 18 to 21 until there are six units. Figures 17-20 show the next few steps of this progression. As in RAW, your thread path will alternate with each unit.

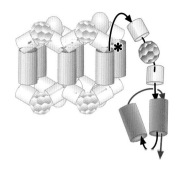

figure 17

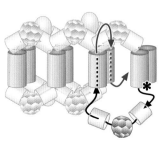

figure 18

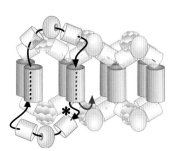

figure 19

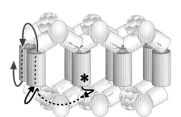

figure 20

The Bridges

22 After completing Row 1, weave through Group 2 and ladder up to Group 1. Pick up two bugles and ladder stitch them together one time side-by-side (figure 21). Pick up Group 1. Pick up two bugles and ladder stitch them together side-by-side one time (figure 22).

25 Pick up two bugles and ladder them together. Pick up Group 1 and two bugles, then ladder stitch the two bugles together. Stitch through the first Group 1 (figures 25 and 26).

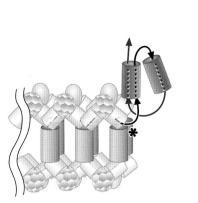

figure 21

figure 22

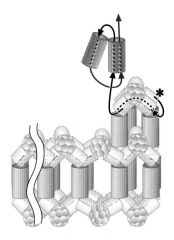

figure 25

23 Still referring to figure 22, sew through the existing Group 1 from the previous unit. Ladder down to Group 2 below without adding any beads.

24 Flip the beadwork. With the needle coming out of an existing Group 2, sew through the next bugle. Pick up one Group 2 and sew through the next bugle (figure 23). Sew through the first Group 2, then the bugle, and the second Group 2. Ladder up to Group 1 (figure 24).

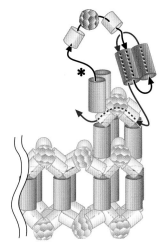

figure 26

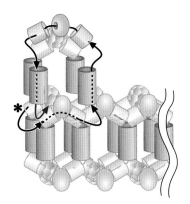

figure 23

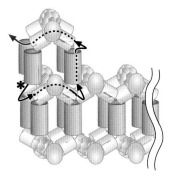

figure 24

26 Flip the beadwork over and ladder through the adjacent Group 2 without adding any beads. Stitch through the next bugle, then pick up one Group 2. Stitch through the next bugle, the first Group 2, and the next bugle. Then ladder down to the adjacent bugle without adding any beads (figure 27).

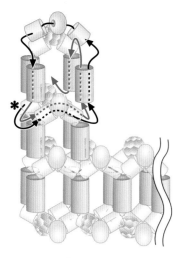

figure 27

Row 2

27 Pick up a Group 1 and two bugles, then ladder together the bugles (figure 28).

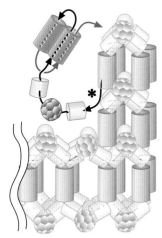

figure 28

28 Pick up a Group 1 and stitch through the next bugle. Ladder up through the adjacent bugle without adding any beads (figure 29).

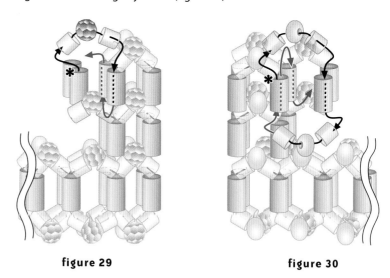

figure 29   **figure 30**

29 Pick up a Group 2 and stitch through a bugle. Pick up another Group 2 and stitch through the next bugle. Ladder down through the adjacent bugle without adding any beads (figure 30).

30 Once completed, weave the needle through the bottom Group 1 and the front bugle (facing the same way as rows 1–6). Follow steps 18 to 21, creating six RAW pieces total (the first square will already exist from the previous row.)

Make The Next Bridge

31 Using figure 31 as a guide for the next two steps, weave the needle all the way around the back and ladder up to Group 1 without adding any beads, so that the needle is coming out of the top Group 1 parallel to the bottom row and facing into the unconnected side.

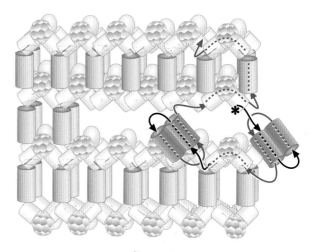

figure 31

32 Pick up two bugles and ladder stitch them together. Sew through the existing Group 1 on the first square created. Pick up two bugles and ladder stitch together. Sew through the existing Group 1 on the previous unit.

Rows and Bridges

33 Once completed, move the needle to the shorter side of the rectangle on the end. Repeat steps 22 to 30.

34 Repeat steps 31 and 32.

35 Continue doing this until there are 13 rows and 12 pairs of bridges between them.

Zip The Tube

Refer to figure 32 for steps 36 through 39

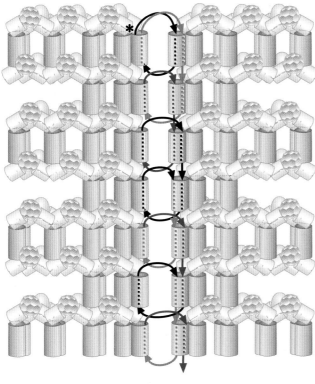

figure 32

36 Fold the completed piece together lengthwise so that the bugle beads line up. Place the rope in the middle.

37 Use an existing thread or add thread (you need about an arm-length).

38 On the outside rows only, ladder stitch the bugle beads between the top and bottom opening all the way across. Do not add any beads while doing this.

39 Once completed, weave in the thread, tie half-hitch knots, and end it.

Side Rings

40 Thread the needle with one arm-length of thread, leaving a six-inch (15.2 cm) tail.

41 Pick up 20 Delicas and thread the needle through the first three make a circle.

42 Use even-count tubular peyote stitch for five rows. Once completed, weave in the tail, tie half-hitch knots, and end it. Go back to the working thread.

43 Move the needle down one Delica bead on the diagonal in the base. Stitch in each ditch all the way around with 15° seed beads (figure 33).

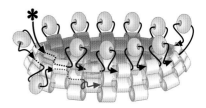

figure 33

44 Again move the needle down one Delica bead on the diagonal in the base and stitch in the ditch, this time alternating 2-mm round crystals and 15° seed beads all the way around (figure 34).

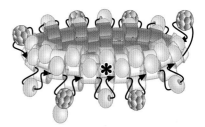

figure 34

45 Repeat step 43.

46 With the tube positioned in the exact middle of the rope, slip a ring onto the rope, equidistant from each of the two ends of the tube. Leave about 16 to 20 rows for the tube to be able to slide between the two rings. Tack down the ring using the remaining thread. Weave in the thread, tie half-hitch knots, and end it.

47 Repeat steps 41 to 46 to make and attach the second side ring.

Centerpiece

48 Thread the needle with one and a half arm-lengths of thread and leave an 8-inch (20.3 cm) tail.

49 Pick up 36 Delicas and run the needle through the first three to create a circle.

50 After using even-count peyote stitch for five rows, thread the tail. Weave it to the center of the peyote stitch circle and pierce it through to the middle. Pick up the 14-mm pearl. Sew through the pearl and the peyote stitch on the opposite side of the circle. Reinforce once by weaving through the pearl again.

51 Weave in the thread, tie half-hitch knots, and end it.

52 Go back to the working thread. Move the needle down one Delica on the diagonal in the base. Tie a half-hitch knot. Pick up one 2-mm round crystal and stitch in the ditch. Pick up one 15° seed bead and stitch in the next ditch. Continue alternating one round crystal and one 15° in each ditch until completing the row.

53 After completing the first row of ditches, move the needle down one Delica bead on the diagonal. Start the next row by stitching in each ditch with one 15°.

54 Repeat step 53.

55 Weave the needle to a middle 15° of choice. Pick up five 15° seed beads and thread the needle through a bugle in the center tube. Pick up five more 15°s and run the needle back through the 15° in the centerpiece. Reinforce it several times.

56 Weave in the thread, tie half-hitch knots, and end it.

The Clasp

57 Follow the directions on page 19 to make a Standard Clasp.

58 To attach the ring clasp, come out at one end of the rope and pick up three 11° seed beads. Sew through two beads in the middle row of the ring. Pick up five 11° seed beads. Sew back through the opposite side of the end of the rope. Weave the needle through the RAW and back through the attachment to reinforce.

Attach the Toggle

59 Use an existing thread at the opposite end of the rope, or add 18 inches (45.7 cm) of thread. Pick up five 11° seed beads. Sew through two Delicas in the middle of the toggle. Pick up five 11° seed beads. Sew back through the opposite side of the end of the rope. Weave the needle through the RAW and back through the attachment to reinforce.

GALLERY

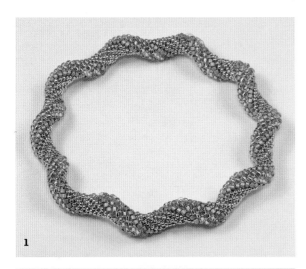

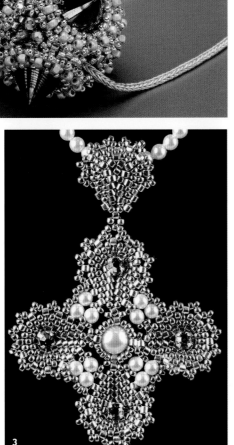

1 MET INNMON
Kudu Spiral Bangle, 2009
8 x 8 cm
Seed beads; kudu spiral stitch
Photography by Larry Hansen

5 LAURA MCCABE
Psilomalene Mace Pendant, 2007
3 x 3 x 3 cm
24-karat gold plated seed beads, custom-cut psilomalene points, cubic
zirconia beads, 22-karat gold chain; peyote stitch, embellishment
Photography by Melinda Holden

3 GLENDA PAUNONEN
Ravenna Cross, 2012
1.9 x 8.8 cm
Pearls, cylinder beads, rose montees; peyote stitch
Photography by Jaani Turunen

4 HANNAH ROSNER
Royal Ruffles Ribbon Bracelet, 2013
2.5 x 1.3 x 17.8 cm
Seed beads; peyote stitch
Photography by artist

1 LAURA MCCABE
Diamonds in the Rough Bracelet, 2010
17 x 2 cm
Glass seed beads, stainless-steel jam nuts, crystals, freshwater pearls;
peyote stitch, embellishment
Photography by Melinda Holden

2 LAURA MCCABE
Etruscan Bracelet, 2007
17 x 5 cm
Custom-cut kambaba jasper stone points, 24-karat gold plated seed beads,
crystal beads, 14-karat gold clasp; peyote stitch, embellishment
Photography by Melinda Holden

3 MELISSA GRAKOWSKY SHIPPEE
Saraswati Necklace, 2011
32 x 33 x 1 cm
Seed beads, crystal beads, crystal stones, wire; right-angle weave
Photography by artist

4 MELISSA GRAKOWSKY SHIPPEE
Song of the Siren, 2012
38 x 34 x 1 cm
Seed beads, crystal beads, crystal stones; peyote stitch, fringing
Photography by artist

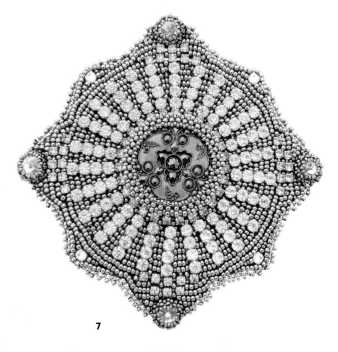

5 AMY BLEVINS
Looking Glass, 2013
Pendant: 4 x 2.5 x 1.5 cm
Crystal rivoli, Japanese seed beads, crystal round beads, rulla beads, Czech glass lentil beads, pearl beads, sterling-silver clasp and wire; herringbone stitch, peyote stitch, crimping
Photography by George Boulton

6 CARRIE JOHNSON
Golden Plumeria, 2013
63 x 7.5 x 2 cm
Venetian glass beads, seed beads; cubic right-angle weave, peyote stitch
Photography by artist

7 LIZ THOMPSON
St. George Medallion, 2013
10 x 10 x 1 cm
Seed beads, crystal rivolis, vintage crystals, Czech button; right-angle weave, bead embroidery
Photography by artist

1 MELISSA GRAKOWSKY SHIPPEE
Bollywood Necklace, 2010
32 x 30 x 1 cm
Seed beads, crystal beads, crystal stones; peyote stitch, netting, right-angle weave
Photography by artist

2 PAULETTE BARON
Spike Me!, 2013
7.6 x 10.6 x 4.4 cm
Seed beads, cylinder beads, hex beads, glass drop beads, glass spikes, suede-like material, wire textile; flat peyote stitch, brick stitch
Photography by Carrie Johnson

3

4

5

3 GLENDA PAUNONEN
Nepal Bracelet, 2010
0.6 x 2.5 x 45.7 cm
Cylinder beads, crystals; peyote stitch
Photography by Jaani Turunen

4 LIISA TURUNEN
Windows of Sainte Chapelle, 2012
0.5 x 2.7 x 18 cm
Seed beads, cylinder beads, crystals; peyote stitch,
right-angle weave
Photography by Jaani Turunen

5 SHERRY SERAFINI
Lazy River, 2013
17.8 x 5.1 cm
Seed beads; bead embroidery
Photography by artist

About the Author

Amy Katz is a nationally recognized teacher and designer with a passion for sharing her love of working with seed beads. Amy's signature style and vision are to give a fine jewelry look to her designs using seed beads, crystals, pearls, and other elegant materials. Visit Amy's website and see her latest creations and instructions at www.beadjourney.com.

Acknowledgments & Dedication

As a bead artist, I find no greater privilege than being able to communicate my joy of creating. I am so very grateful for the opportunity to work on this book. To all of the artists and friends who have been part of this process, I extend my deepest gratitude for your dedication and talents.

Paulette Baron, bead artist and graphic artist extraordinaire, spent hours illustrating this book. Carrie Johnson made the jewelry come to life with her exceptional photos. And of course, Melissa Grakowsky Shippee did a sensational job keeping the technical editing on track.

Thank you to the following artists for testing projects: Dana Colbert for Daisy Darling Necklace, Susan Marks for Perfect Touch Earrings, Barb Boyd for Bejeweled Barrel Bracelet, Sherry Ellis for Animal Instinct Bracelet, Kristen Ho for Girls' Night Out Necklace, and Susan Etkind for Reflections Pendant. And Susan, thank you again for creating the Opposites Attract Bracelet.

I would also like to extend my gratitude to all of the wonderful artists who have lent photos of their art for the gallery, as well as to the staff at Lark Books.

Thank you to Rick, Andrew, and Melissa for being a part of this process and coping with my "ups and downs" as I created each piece of jewelry. You were there when projects came together and on those occasions when they fell apart, and your support helped me create and move forward to complete this work.

And finally I extend a special thank you to the bead community. If it weren't for all of you and your inspiration, there would be no book and no way for the art to live on. This book is dedicated to you.

Index